KU-165-755

THE COMPLETE
STITCH DIRECTORY

◆

Knitting, Crochet,
Embroidery and
Needlepoint

THE COMPLETE
STITCH
DIRECTORY

◆

Knitting, Crochet,
Embroidery and
Needlepoint

CHANCELLOR
PRESS

Executive Manager	Susan Egerton-Jones
Design Manager	Hans Verkroost
Editor	Patsy North
Designer	Sue Hall
Consultants	Linda Seward
	Penny Hill
	Marilyn Wilson
	Sue Hopper
	Margaret Tucker
Translation	Sheilagh Sainsbury Brown
Production	Peter Phillips
	Stewart Bowling

Edited and designed by the Artists House
Division of Mitchell Beazley International Ltd
part of Reed International Books

Text and illustrations from the work "Millepunti"
© 1982 Gruppo Editoriale Fabbri S.p.A. Milan
Additional pictures © 1988 Mitchell Beazley Publishers
Additional text and translation © 1988 Mitchell Beazley
Publishers
The work "The Complete Stitch Directory" © 1988
Reed International Books Ltd

All rights reserved. No part of this work may be
reproduced or utilized in any form by any means,
electronic or mechanical, including photocopying,
recording or by any information storage and retrieval
system, without the prior written permission of the publisher.

The publishers have made every effort to ensure that all
instructions given in this book are accurate and safe, but
they cannot accept liability for any resulting injury, damage
or loss to either person or property whether direct or
consequential and howsoever arising. The author and
publishers will be grateful for any information which will
assist them in keeping future editions up to date.

ISBN 1 85152 230 1

Printed in Malaysia

CONTENTS

INTRODUCTION

The Complete Stitch Directory is an invaluable reference book and source of inspiration for everyone interested in knitting, crochet and embroidery. These traditional crafts remain as popular today as they have ever been and they continue to attract new enthusiasts who appreciate the beautiful quality of hand-made items and would like to acquire the skills necessary to create them themselves. Manufacturers are responding to this enthusiasm by producing an ever-expanding range of yarns and threads, increasingly using unusual blends of colours and fibres, both natural and man-made, so that the possibilities for creating exciting designs in knitwear, crochet work and embroidery have never been better. It takes only one visit to a well-stocked yarn shop to make one's fingers start itching to begin a new piece of work.

The Complete Stitch Directory provides a wealth of material for those who wish to explore the crafts of knitting, crochet and embroidery more fully, whether to brush up on their technical knowledge or to pursue design ideas of their own. The book is divided into three main sections covering the basics as well as some of the more unusual techniques of each craft and each containing a comprehensive library of stitches, beautifully photographed in full colour to show all the detail clearly. Full pattern instructions are given with each stitch.

The knitting and crochet sections begin with a thorough explanation of basic techniques with the aid of detailed diagrams, so that beginners can learn the groundwork while those with more expertise can refresh their memories about the various methods of increasing and decreasing, making neat edgings and borders and working in the round. In addition, traditional and rather more complicated techniques such as Aran knitting, filet crochet and Irish lace are included, with working diagrams and examples of the stitches and patterns which can be made.

The stitch collection in the knitting and crochet sections contains a wide range of patterns suitable for many different effects. For a delicate fabric, choose from the eyelet stitches or the lacy stitches or incorporate beads into the work, while for a chunky look, find inspiration from the knitted cables or the relief crochet. Some stunning effects can also be achieved by mixing shades of yarn and following one of the many multi-coloured patterns.

The collection of stitches will provide ideas for anyone interested in designing their own knit and crochet wear and can also be used to adapt a standard commercial pattern to create a completely original garment. To do this, select a new stitch that will suit the basic style of the garment and the type of yarn suggested for it: for example, a T-shaped sweater knitted in a chunky wool might look more interesting worked in one of the Aran patterns. Then experiment with the tension of the new stitch to make sure that it will match the tension of the original pattern. In this way, the garment will work up with the correct measurements. For beginners, it is best to use a simple shape so that the chosen stitch makes the impact rather than the detailed styling of the garment. Many of the knitting and crochet stitches can also be used for items around the home such as cot covers, blankets, travel rugs and cushions. Although size is not so critical here, select a stitch that is appropriate to the weight of yarn and the purpose for which it will be used.

The embroidery and needlepoint section of *The Complete Stitch Directory* encompasses a wide variety of stitches and methods from the basics of free embroidery to the more disciplined techniques of counted thread work such as Assisi work and Hardanger embroidery. It explains in detail how to work stem stitches, chain stitches, feather stitches and many more, with the aid of photographs showing the correct needle position. Other areas of embroidery covered are drawn thread work and smocking, with explanations of how to prepare the fabric and a selection of suitable stitches to use. Appliqué and beadwork are also

included and the section concludes with a colourful collection of needlepoint stitches, including some of the beautiful Florentine patterns.

In order to make *The Complete Stitch Directory* easy to use, each section is coded with the appropriate symbol for knitting, crochet, embroidery or needlepoint. This will be found at the top of each page, together with the type of technique or family of stitches and the name of each individual stitch on that page, making a useful reference when glancing through the book. In addition, there is a contents list for each section and a comprehensive index, so that any stitch or technique can be quickly located. For example, to find a selection of lacy stitches to use in a crochet design, look for this group of stitches in the contents list for the crochet section. This will refer you to six pages of lacy stitches to choose from.

So add *The Complete Stitch Directory* to your library – whether you are already a crafts enthusiast or a beginner about to embark on a new and rewarding pastime, you will refer to it again and again.

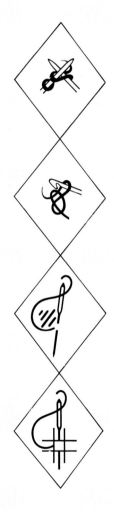

INTRODUCTION
— TO —
KNITTING

This knitting section presents a wealth of inspirational stitch patterns, ranging from delicate lacy stitches and multi-coloured designs full of visual impact to the heavily textured effects of cable knitting. It also explains all the basic techniques that a knitter may need to refer to when working a pattern.

Materials

Needles Knitting needles are used in pairs or sets. They are machine-made of aluminium, steel, plastic or wood in varying lengths and are graded in seventeen international sizes from 2mm to 17mm.

Double-pointed needles are sold in sets of four or six, sized in the same way as ordinary needles. They are used for knitting in the round, either for tubular shapes such as socks, gloves or sweater sleeves or for flat rounds such as shawls.

Circular needles are a pair of pointed needles joined by a flexible length of wire or plastic. They are made in various sizes and lengths and are used for large tubular shapes such as sweaters or skirts.

Cable needles are very short double-pointed needles and come in just a few sizes. They are used for holding stitches while working a cable.

Yarns There are many types and weights of yarn, made of natural or man-made fibres or a mixture of both. However, you can knit with anything, as long as it is flexible, even strips of fabric, ribbons and string.

Tension

Always work a stitch sample to check your tension before making any garment. The tension is given at the beginning of a pattern. Knit a sample at least 15cm (6in) square, using the correct yarn, needles and pattern.

Measuring the stitches Lay the sample on a flat surface. Place pins vertically 10cm (4in) apart and then count the stitches between them.

Measuring the rows Lay the sample on a flat surface. Place pins horizontally 10cm (4in) apart and then count the rows between them.

If there are too many stitches and rows, try a size larger needle. If there are too few stitches and rows, try a size finer needle.

Abbreviations

beg	beginning
C2L	K 2nd stitch through back of loop, then K 1st stitch and slip off needle together
C2R	K 2nd stitch, then K 1st stitch and slip off needle together
C3B(P)	slip 1 stitch onto cable needle, hold at back of work, K2 then P1 from cable needle
C3F(K)	slip 2 stitches onto cable needle, hold at front of work, K1 then K2 from cable needle
C3F(P)	slip 2 stitches onto cable needle, hold at front of work, P1 then K2 from cable needle
C4B	slip 2 stitches onto cable needle, hold at back of work, K2 then K2 from cable needle
C4F	slip 2 stitches onto cable needle, hold at front of work, K2 then K2 from cable needle
dec	decrease

foll	following
inc	increase
K	knit
K-wise	knitwise
K1D	K into next stitch, 1 row down
make 1	yarn forward between K stitches
	yarn over needle between a P and a K stitch
	yarn round needle between P stitches or between a K and a P stitch
make 2	yarn round needle twice
P	purl
P-wise	purlwise
patt	pattern
PC2R	P 2nd stitch, then P 1st stitch and slip off needle together
psso	pass slipped stitch over
p2sso	pass 2 slipped stitches over
rem	remaining
rep	repeat
RS	right side
sl1	slip 1 knitwise
sl1 P	slip 1 purlwise
st st	stocking stitch

T2L	P 2nd stitch through back of loop, then K 1st stitch and slip off needle together
T2R	K 2nd stitch, then P 1st stitch and slip off needle together
tbl	through back of loop(s)
tog	together
wk	work
WS	wrong side
ybk	yarn back
yfwd	yarn forward
yon	yarn over needle
ytf	yarn to front
yrn	yarn round needle

The instructions given between two asterisks * are repeated to the end of the row, or to the next instructions given.

Example 1: Row 1 *K1, P1*. This means repeat K1, P1 to the end of the row.

Example 2: Row 1 *K2, P3*, end with K2. This means repeat K2, P3 to the last 2 stitches, then K2.

Work instructions within brackets ( ) the number of times stated.

Casting on

Casting on with one needle
Casting on with two needles
Casting on with two needles: twisted method

Casting on with one needle 1. Take the yarn in the left hand and pull a length three times longer than is needed to work with. With the thumb and first finger of the left hand, make a loop.

2. Holding the needle in the right hand, insert it through the loop from below. With the first finger of the right hand, wind the yarn from the ball under and over the needle from left to right.

3. With the first finger of the left hand slip the loop over the needle point, withdraw the finger and tighten the loop. The first stitch is made. Repeat for each stitch.

Casting on with two needles 1. Make the first stitch as in the previous method. Put it on the left-hand needle. Hold one needle in each hand. Insert the right-hand needle into the stitch and wind the yarn up and over the needle.

2. Draw the right-hand needle back a little and make the second stitch by pulling the left-hand needle up and drawing the yarn through the first stitch.

3. Put the second stitch onto the left-hand needle and continue making stitches with the right-hand needle and passing them onto the left-hand needle until the desired number of stitches are worked.

Casting on with two needles: twisted method 1. Pull a length of yarn to work with. Make a loop with the thumb and first finger of the left hand and insert the needle into it. Wind the working yarn over and under the needle from the left.

2. Hold the working yarn with the left hand, and the yarn coming from the ball in the right. Wind the latter under and over the needle from the right.

3. Lift the first loop over the second, using the left-hand needle. This makes the first stitch. Continue in this way until the desired number of stitches are worked.

Double casting on: 1st method 1. This forms a casing through which ribbon or elastic may later be threaded. It requires a special method of casting on. Cast on half the number of stitches finally required, using a colour different from that of the work.

2. With the working yarn work the first row in the following way: Knit one stitch, bring the yarn to the front of the work, making a stitch (because the yarn will pass over the right-hand needle to work the next stitch).

3. Knit into the next stitch and then yarn forward to make a stitch. Repeat these two actions to the end of the row, ending up with double the number of stitches.

4. On the return row, slip purlwise the made stitches, without working them, holding the yarn to the back of the work. Purl the stitches which were previously knitted.

5. Now slip the purl stitches of the previous row, and taking the yarn to the back, knit the stitches slipped in the previous row.

6. Work like this for four or five rows, then continue normally in 1/1 rib and the selected stitch. Finally unravel the different colour cast-on edge.

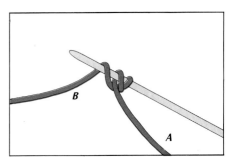

Double casting on: 2nd method 1. With the working yarn **A**, make the first stitch on the needle. Then take yarn **B** round the needle, passing it from the front, over the needle and back down.

2. With the right hand take yarn **A** under the needle from back to front, holding it firm. In this way the second stitch is made.

3. With the left hand take yarn **B** over the needle again from front to back, as before.

Casting on
Double casting on, continued
Casting on with four needles
Casting on with a circular needle

4. With the right hand take yarn **A** from front to back under the needle, so making the third stitch. Continue in this way until the required number of stitches have been made.

5. On the following row knit into the knit stitches and slip the purl as set. Do not work the last stitch.

6. Work another four or five rows in this way, then start normal 1/1 ribbing. At the end of the work, carefully pull the loop made by the unworked stitch and draw out the starting yarn.

**Casting on with four needles: 1st method
1.** On each of the four double-ended needles, cast on a quarter of the total stitches. Having completed one needle, lay the second alongside the first, with the point slightly protruding. Continue in this way with the other needles.

2. Having cast on the last stitch, mark this point with a marker thread of a different colour knotted through the stitch. Each round will start here.

3. Start working with a fifth needle taking care at the first and last stitches, pulling the yarn tight to avoid a hole forming at the start or end of the work. At the end of the first round, the marker thread shows the start of the second.

**Casting on with four needles: 2nd method
1.** This is used to work a flat piece of work starting at the centre. With a crochet hook make a chain of eight stitches (or a number divisible by four) and pick these up with the needles.

2. Slip two stitches onto each needle. Continue working, increasing one stitch between each group of two on the first round, and increasing two stitches at the centre of each section on the following rounds.

Casting on with a circular needle Cast on the number of stitches required for the work, then at the start of the work knot a marker thread of a contrasting colour through the stitch. Each round starts here. Keep the last stitch on the right-hand point and work the round from the left.

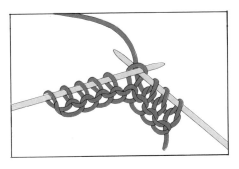

Knit or plain stitch 1. Keep the needle holding the stitches in the left hand and with the yarn held firmly behind the needle, insert the right-hand needle into the next stitch from front to back.

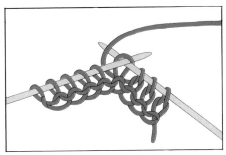

2. With the first finger of the right hand take the yarn around the point of the right-hand needle as shown.

3. Withdraw the right-hand needle a little, lifting the yarn through and letting the worked stitch fall from the left-hand needle.

4. Finish the row in this way. The result will be a line of knit stitches on one side of the work and a line of purl on the other. Working alternate rows of knit and purl makes stocking stitch, as shown above.

Purl stitch 1. Keeping the needle holding the stitches in the left hand, insert the needle from back to front, with the yarn in front of the needle.

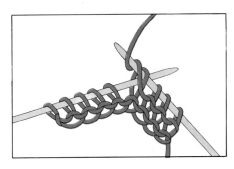

2. Take the working yarn round the needle, coming back to the front under the needle.

3. Lift the yarn through, letting the worked stitch fall from the left-hand needle.

4. Continue in this way to the end of the row. This produces purl stitches on one side of the work and knit on the other. The purl side of stocking stitch can be used as the right side, as shown above. It is then called reverse stocking stitch.

Garter stitch This basic stitch is worked with all rows the same, either all knit or all purl without alternating.

13

Casting off
Casting off: simple method
Casting off with a crochet hook
Casting off double stitches

Casting off: simple method 1. Work two stitches then *pass the point of the left-hand needle into the first of these stitches.

2. Lift the first stitch over the second, carefully lengthening it*.

3. Work another stitch normally and repeat from * to *.

Casting off with a crochet hook: 1st method 1. This method results in a tighter finish. Leave the stitches on the left-hand needle and insert the crochet hook into the first two stitches.

2. *Draw the second stitch through the first. Insert the crochet hook into the next stitch, and repeat from *. In this method the working yarn is not used.

Casting off with a crochet hook: 2nd method This method uses the working yarn, and the tension of the work can be regulated. Insert the crochet hook into the first two stitches, *wind the yarn round the crochet hook, pull it through the stitches. Insert the crochet hook into the next stitch and repeat from *.

Casting off double stitches 1. Insert a needle through the stitches so that they are divided into two groups, slipping the second group alternately onto the second needle. Thread a sewing needle. Thread this through a stitch on the front needle, letting the stitch fall.

2. Thread through the first two stitches on the back needle: enter into the first stitch from behind and come out through the next stitch from the inside. Let them both fall.

3. *Return to the front needle, re-entering the first stitch (the one just dropped) and coming out through the next stitch as shown, letting it fall.

Casting off

Casting off double stitches, continued Finishing the work
Casting off joining two pieces Darning in vertically
Darning in horizontally

4. Return to the back needle, re-enter from behind the stitch previously dropped, come out through the next stitch and let it fall*. Repeat from * to *.

Casting off double stitches from one needle 1. The previous method can be worked leaving the stitches on one needle. Insert the threaded sewing needle into the first stitch from behind, then through the second, letting them fall.

2. *Re-enter the first stitch from behind and out through the third stitch. Enter the second stitch from behind and out through the fourth*. Continue in this way, always taking two stitches.

Casting off joining two pieces 1. This is worked on the wrong side. Keep the pieces to be joined on two needles, right sides together. With a third needle knit together the first stitch from each needle, making a single stitch.

2. *Knit together the next two stitches, one from each needle, making a second stitch. Slip the first stitch over the second*.

3. Repeat from * to * to the end of the row. This method achieves two sections of work cast off with one seam. It is widely used to finish shoulder seams.

Finishing the work At the end of the last row cut the yarn, passing it through the last stitch to prevent unravelling.

Darning in vertically Thread a sewing needle with the working yarn and weave in and out of the row ends for about 4cm (1½in).

Darning in horizontally Work as explained for vertical finishing off, weaving through the nearest edge, usually the seam edge.

Stitches for shape and pattern

Twisted stitches   Making a stitch
Slipped stitches   Slipped stitch decreasing

Twisted knit or plain stitch Make a knit stitch in the normal way, but knit into the back of the stitch making the work less elastic as the stitches are twisted.

Twisted purl stitch Work a purl stitch, bringing the needle through the back of the loop to the front, twisting the stitch.

Slip stitch knitwise With the yarn to the back of the work, enter a stitch as though to knit it and slip it onto the right-hand needle without doing so.

Slip stitch purlwise With the yarn to the front, enter the stitch as though to purl it and slip it onto the right-hand needle without doing so.

Making a stitch between knit stitches Bring the yarn to the front, then over the needle to the back and continue working. On the return row work the made stitch normally.

Making a stitch between purl stitches Take the yarn to the back of the work over the needle, then to the front again, and continue working. On the return row work the made stitch as a normal stitch.

Making a stitch between a knit and a purl stitch Having worked a knit stitch, bring the yarn forward under the right-hand needle, then wind it over the needle and back to the front. Purl the next stitch.

Slipped stitches, single decrease Slip one stitch and work the following. With the left-hand needle lift the unworked stitch over the worked stitch, letting it fall.

Slipped stitches, double decrease Slip one stitch without working it, work the next two together and pass the slipped stitch over and let it fall.

Single elongated stitch Insert the needle into the stitch in the row below the one that should be worked next. Knit it.

Double elongated stitch Insert the needle into the stitch four or more rows below the one that should be worked next, letting the stitch on the needle fall and run down. Knit it. This is used in stitches with a honeycomb effect.

Elongated stitch using a crochet hook This is a variation of the previous example. Instead of using the needle, insert the crochet hook several rows below and draw through a loop, which is then knitted with the next stitch.

Elongated stitches: alternative method **1.** Wind the yarn round the needle at least three times for each stitch. Then knit into the next stitch.

2. On the next row, on either the right or wrong side of the work, work the stitches normally letting the extra loops drop off the needle. Long stitches formed in this way are generally used in lacy bands between solid areas.

Cross two stitches right, knitting Knit into the front of the second stitch on the left-hand needle, but do not drop the stitch off. Then knit into the front of the first stitch and let them drop off the needle together.

Cross two stitches left, knitting Knit into the back of the second stitch on the left-hand needle but do not drop the stitch off. Then knit into the back of the first stitch and allow both stitches to drop off the needle together.

Cross two stitches right, purling Purl into the front of the second stitch on the left-hand needle, but do not drop the stitch off. Then purl into the front of the first stitch and let both stitches drop off the needle together.

Cross two stitches left, purling Purl into the front of the second stitch on the left-hand needle from behind the first stitch (held on a cable needle). Then purl into the front of the first stitch and allow to drop off the needle.

Increasing

Knitting into the same stitch twice   Yarn forward method
Invisible increasing   Extending a row
Raised increasing   Increasing at edges

Knitting into the same stitch twice This method of increasing can be worked in several ways. On a knit row, knit into the same stitch twice, first into the front of the stitch and then into the back, letting it fall from the left-hand needle. On a purl row, purl first into the front and then into the back of the stitch.

Invisible increasing Before working the stitch on the needle, work the one below in the previous row, then work into the back of the first one. This method can also be used on a purl row.

Raised increasing 1. In this method the horizontal bar between two stitches is worked.

2. Pick up this bar with the right-hand needle and slip it onto the left, twisting it as you do so. This method can also be used on a purl row and is almost invisible if the stitch is worked into the back.

Yarn forward method This is the simplest way of increasing a stitch in the work. Bring the yarn forward between the needles on a knit row and then knit into the next stitch. On the return row work this stitch normally. For increasing on a purl row, see page 16.

Extending a row Cast on the required number of stitches at the beginning or end of a row by the method normally used.

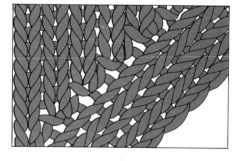

Simple increasing at edges Use the first method described above for increasing within a row, ie. knit twice into the same stitch. In paired increasing, when increasing is worked three stitches from the end on the right-hand edge, it must be made four stitches from the end of the left-hand edge.

Invisible increasing at edges Use the invisible increasing method described above, ie. work an increase by inserting the needle into the stitch in the previous row and working into it. Paired increasing is achieved by working into the stitch below the third stitch from the beginning and the end of a row.

Simple moss increasing at edges Work a knit stitch normally, but without letting it drop from the needle. Bring the yarn to the front and purl into the same stitch. For paired increasing, increase three stitches in from the right-hand edge and on the fourth stitch from the end of the row.

Simple raised increasing at edges Lift the horizontal bar between the right and left-hand needles and knit into the back of it. Paired increasing is achieved by working into the horizontal bar after the third stitch from the start of the row and before the third stitch from the end of the row.

Simple barred increasing at edges Work into the back loop of the stitch from the previous row and then into the stitch on the needle. Paired increasing is achieved by increasing into the stitch below the third stitch from the start of the row and into the stitch below the third stitch from the end of the row.

Lace increasing at edges Increase by taking the yarn forward and over the needle and working it on the following row, making a small hole. Paired increasing is achieved by taking the yarn forward and over the needle after the third stitch from the start of the row and before the third stitch from the end of the row.

Double bar increasing Knit into the front and back of the stitch before a centre stitch, then knit into the front and back of the centre stitch.

Double invisible increasing In the stitch before the centre stitch, make an invisible increasing stitch left. Knit the centre stitch and then make an invisible increasing stitch right.

Double moss increasing Knit and purl into the stitch before the centre stitch, knit the centre stitch, and then knit and purl into the next stitch.

Double raised increasing Knit into the horizontal thread before the centre stitch, knit the centre stitch and then knit into the next horizontal thread.

Double invisible increasing into one stitch Knit into the loop below the centre stitch, then knit into the back of the centre stitch and knit again into the loop below the centre stitch.

Double lace increasing Take the yarn forward and over the needle, knit the centre stitch and take the yarn forward and over the needle again. Work the loops normally on the next row.

Decreasing
Knit decreasing   Slip stitch decreasing
Purl decreasing   Decreasing at edges

Knit decreasing This is the simplest and most commonly used method. Knit two stitches together, making one.

Purl decreasing Purl next two stitches together, making one.

Slip stitch decreasing Slip a stitch from the left-hand needle onto the right-hand needle. Knit normally into the next stitch and pass the slipped stitch over it.

Knit decreasing inside a border of two stitches, sloping to the left Using the slip stitch decreasing described above, slip the third stitch over the fourth.

Knit decreasing inside a border of two stitches, sloping to the right Using the knit decreasing method described above, knit the fourth and third stitches from the end together.

Alternative method With a left slope use purl decreasing on the wrong side of work. With a right slope use knit decreasing on the right side of work, working into the back of the stitch. Symmetry is achieved by working together the fourth and third stitches at the end of either the knit or purl rows.

Decorative decreasing Whether the slope is to the left or to the right, purl the stitches. Symmetry is achieved by working together the third and fourth stitches at either end of a row.

Lacy decreasing Work a left slope on the wrong side of the work and a right slope on the right side of the work in the following way: work until there are five stitches left on the needle. Slip two stitches onto right-hand needle, lift second stitch over first. Slip stitch back onto left-hand needle and work to end.

Double slip stitch decreasing Slip one stitch, knit the next two together and pass the slipped stitch over the resulting stitch.

Decreasing/Edgings and borders
Double decreasing
Plain, purled and cabled edgings
Garter stitch, moss stitch and 1/1 ribbed borders

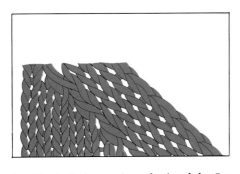

Double knit decreasing, sloping left On the right side of the work, knit three stitches together through the back of the loops.

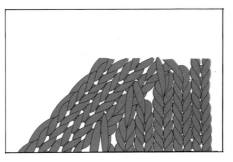

Double knit decreasing, sloping right On the right side of the work, knit three stitches together normally.

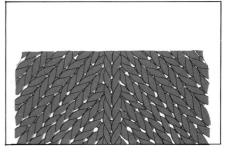

Decreasing on a central line Slip two stitches knitwise, passing the needle first through the second and then through the first, from left to right. Knit into the next stitch, and then pass the two slipped stitches over the knitted stitch.

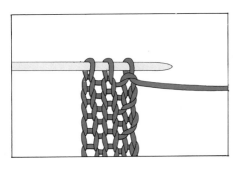

Plain edging Use this method for making an invisible seam. With right side of work facing, knit into the back of the first and last stitch. On the wrong side of work purl the first stitch and slip the last stitch without working it.

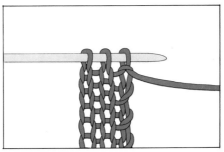

Purled edging Use this method for normal seams. On either a purl or a knit row, slip the first stitch knitwise without working it and knit into the last stitch.

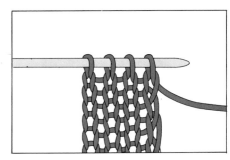

Cabled edging Use this method when stitches are to be picked up later. With right side facing, slip the first stitch knitwise without working it and knit into the last stitch. On wrong side slip the first stitch purlwise without working it and purl into the last stitch.

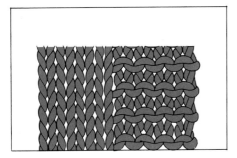

Garter stitch border This is used to finish sections of work done in stocking stitch. Work into the back of the knit stitches forming the border, making the border a firm, integral part of the work.

Moss stitch border This is also used to finish the edge of a section of work done in stocking stitch and is an integral part of the work. Work the border stitches in moss stitch.

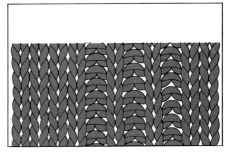

1/1 ribbed border This is another example of a worked-in border. Work the border in 1/1 rib over an odd number of stitches, working two knit stitches at the edge.

Ribbed stitches

Simple 1/1 rib   Twisted 1/1 rib
2/2 rib   7/3 flat rib
Simple purled rib   Double purled rib

Simple 1/1 rib This is the simplest and most widely used of the rib stitches, and is worked over an even number of sts. *Row 1* *K1, P1*. *Row 2* *K1, P1*. Rep these 2 rows.

Twisted 1/1 rib This a variation of simple 1/1 rib, the only difference being that the knit stitches are worked into the back of the stitch, resulting in a firmer fabric.

2/2 rib Work over a number of sts divisible by 4. *Row 1* *K2, P2*. *Row 2* *K2, P2*. Rep these 2 rows.

7/3 flat rib Work over a number of sts divisible by 10. *Row 1* *K7, P3*. *Row 2* *K3, P7*. Rep these 2 rows. The width of this type of rib can be varied.

Simple purled rib Work over a number of sts divisible by 5 + 2. *Row 1* *P2, K1, P1, K1*, end with P2. *Row 2* *K2, P3*, end with K2. Rep these 2 rows.

Double purled rib Work over a number of sts divisible by 7 + 3. *Row 1 (RS)* P3, *K1, P1, K2, P3*. *Row 2* K3, *P2, K1, P1, K3*. *Row 3* P3, *K2, P1, K1, P3*. *Row 4* K3, *P1, K1, P2, K3*. Rep these 4 rows.

Ribbed stitches

English rib   Mock English rib
Slip stitch rib   Slipped moss stitch rib
Irish rib   Piqué rib

English rib Work over an even number of sts. *Row 1* *Make 1, sl1 ybk, K1*. *Row 2* *Make 1, sl1, K2 tog (work tog made and slipped stitch of previous row)*. Rep these 2 rows.

Mock English rib Work over a number of sts divisible by 4. *Row 1* *K3, P1*. *Row 2* *K2, P1, K1*. Rep these 2 rows.

Slip stitch rib Work over a number of sts divisible by 5 + 2. *Row 1* *P2, K1, sl1 P ybk, K1*, end with P2. *Row 2* *K2, P3*, end with K2. Rep these 2 rows.

Slipped moss stitch rib Work on a number of sts divisible by 5. *Row 1* *K1, P1, K1, P1, K1*. *Row 2* *Sl1 P yfwd, P1, K1, P1, K1*. Rep these 2 rows.

Irish rib Work over a number of sts divisible by 3. *Row 1* P. *Row 2 (RS)* *K1, K2tog*. *Row 3* Sl1 P yfwd (the K2tog of previous row), K1*. Rep the last 2 rows.

Piqué rib Work over a number of sts divisible by 10. *Row 1* *P3, K1, P3, K3*. *Rows 2 and 3* Work the stitches as set. *Row 4* K. Rep these 4 rows.

Patterns from knit and purl

Moss stitch Work over an even number of sts. *Row 1* *K1, P1*. *Row 2* *P1, K1*. Rep these 2 rows. This stitch has the same appearance on both sides of the work.

Double moss stitch Work over an even number of sts. *Row 1* *K1, P1*. *Row 2* *K1, P1*. *Row 3* *P1, K1*. *Row 4* *P1, K1*. Rep these 4 rows.

Elongated moss stitch Work over an even number of sts. *Rows 1, 2, 5 and 6* K. *Row 3* *K1, P1*. *Rows 4 and 8* Work the stitches as set. *Row 7* *P1, K1*. Rep these 8 rows.

Single seed stitch Work over a number of sts divisible by 4. *Row 1* *K3, P1*. *Row 2 and all even rows* P. *Rows 3 and 7* K. *Row 5* K1, *P1, K3*, end with P1, K2. *Row 9* Rep from row 1.

Half triple seed stitch Work over a number of sts divisible by 7. *Row 1* *P3, K4*. *Row 2* P2, *K3, P4*, end with P2. *Rows 3 and 7* K. *Rows 4 and 8* P. *Row 5* K2, *P3, K4*, end with K2. *Row 6* K3, *P4, K3*, end with P4. *Row 9* Rep from row 1.

Half quadruple seed stitch Work over a number of sts divisible by 6. *Rows 1 and 3* K1, *P1, K5*, end with P1, K4. *Row 2* *P3, K3*. *Rows 4 and 8* P. *Rows 5 and 7* K4, *P1, K5*, end with P1, K1. *Row 6* *K3, P3*. *Row 9* Rep from row 1.

Patterns from knit and purl

Reverse ridge stitch	Ripple stitch
Chequered stitch	Basket stitch
Square stitch	Triangle stitch

Reverse ridge stitch Work over any number of sts. *Row 1* K. *Row 2* P. *Rows 3 and 4* K. *Row 5* P. *Row 6* K. This stitch appears the same on both sides of the work. The bands can be varied in height according to the number of rows left between the knit rows.

Ripple stitch Work over a number of sts divisible by 4 + 1. *Row 1* P. *Row 2* *K1, P3*, end with K1. *Row 3* *P1, K3*, end with P1. *Row 4* As row 2. *Row 5* Rep from row 1.

Chequered stitch Work over a number of sts divisible by 14. *Rows 1 to 10* *K7, P7*. *Rows 11 to 20* *P7, K7*. Rep from row 1.

Basket stitch Work over a number of sts divisible by 14. *Rows 1 and 9* K. *Rows 2 and 10* P. *Rows 3, 5 and 7* *P10, K4*. *Rows 4, 6, and 8* *P4, K10*. *Rows 11, 13 and 15* P3, *K4, P10*, end with K4, P7. *Rows 12, 14 and 16* K7, *P4, K10*, end with P4, K3. *Row 17* Rep from row 1.

Square stitch Work over a number of sts divisible by 10 + 1. *Rows 1 and 7* K. *Rows 2 and 6* P. *Rows 3 and 5* K4, *P3, K7*, end with K4. *Row 4* P4, *K3, P7*, end with P4. *Rows 8 and 10* K2, *P7, K3*, end with K2. *Row 9* P2, *K7, P3*, end with P2. Rep from row 1.

Triangle stitch Work over a number of sts divisible by 12. *Row 1* K1, *P9, K3*, end with K2. *Row 2* P3, *K7, P5*, end with P2. *Row 3* K3, *P5, K7*, end with K4. *Row 4* P5, *K3, P9*, end with P4. *Row 5* K5, *P1, K11*, end K6. *Rows 6 and 12* P. *Row 7* P4, *K3, P9*, end P5. *Row 8* K4, *P5, K7*, end K3. *Row 9* P2, *K7, P5*, end P3. *Row 10* K2, *P9, K3*, end K1. *Row 11* *K11, P1*. Rep from row 1.

Patterns from knit and purl

Simple diagonal stitch   Double diagonal stitch
Large dot stitch   Diamond pattern

Simple diagonal stitch Work over a number of sts divisible by 5. *Row 1* *P1, K4*. *Row 2* P3, *K1, P4*, end with K1, P1. *Row 3* K2, *P1, K4*, end with P1, K2. *Row 4* P1, *K1, P4*, end with K1, P3. *Row 5* *K4, P1*. *Row 6* *P4, K1*. *Row 7* K1, *P1, K4*, end with P1, K3. *Row 8* P2, *K1, P4*, end with K1, P2. *Row 9* K3, *P1, K4*, end with P1, K1. *Row 10* *K1, P4*. *Row 11* Rep from row 1.

Double diagonal stitch Work over a number of sts divisible by 7. *Row 1* *P3, K4*. *Row 2* P3, *K3, P4*, end with K3, P1. *Row 3* K2, *P3, K4*, end with P3, K2. *Row 4* P1, *K3, P4*, end with K3, P3. *Row 5* *K4, P3*. *Row 6* K2, *P4, K3*, end with P4, K1. *Row 7* P2, *K4, P3*, end with K4, P1. *Row 8* *P4, K3*. *Row 9* K1, *P3, K4*, end with P3, K3. *Row 10* P2, *K3, P4*, end with K3, P2. *Row 11* K3, *P3, K4*, end with P3, K1. *Row 12* *K3, P4*. *Row 13* P1, *K4, P3*, end with K4, P2. *Row 14* K1, *P4, K3*, end with P4, K2. *Row 15* Rep from row 1.

Large dot stitch Work over a number of sts divisible by 10. *Row 1* *K7, P3*. *Row 2* K4, *P5, K5*, end with P5, K1. *Row 3* P2, *K3, P7*, end with K3, P5. *Row 4* As row 2. *Row 5* As row 1. *Rows 6 to 10* Work in st st. *Row 11* K2, *P3, K7*, end with P3, K5. *Row 12* P4, *K5, P5*, end with K5, P1. *Row 13* *P7, K3*. *Row 14* P4, *K5, P5*, end with K5, P1. *Row 15* K2, *P3, K7*, end with P3, K5. *Rows 16 to 20* Work in st st. *Row 21* Rep from row 1.

Diamond pattern Work over a number of sts divisible by 14. *Row 1* *(P1, K1) 4 times, K6*. *Row 2* On this and all even rows, work the sts as set. *Rows 3 and 15* *(K1, P1) 3 times, K4, P1, K3*. *Rows 5 and 13* *K2, P1, K1, P1, K4, P1, K1, P1, K2*. *Rows 7 and 11* *K3, P1, K4, (P1, K1) 3 times*. *Row 9* *K6, (K1, P1) 4 times*. *Row 17* Rep from row 1. With this stitch the wrong side of the work can also be used.

Brocade stitch Work over a number of sts divisible by 12 + 1. *Row 1 (RS)* K1, *P1, K9, P1, K1*. *Row 2* K1, *P1, K1, P7, K1, P1, K1*. *Row 3* K1, *P1, K1, P1, K5, (P1, K1) twice*. *Row 4* P1, *(P1, K1) twice, P3, K1, P1, K1, P2*. *Row 5* K1, *K2, (P1, K1) 3 times, P1, K3*. *Row 6* P1, *P3, (K1, P1) twice, K1, P4*. *Row 7* K1, *K4, P1, K1, P1, K5*. *Row 8* As row 6. *Row 9* As row 5. *Row 10* As row 4. *Row 11* As row 3. *Row 12* As row 2. Rep these 12 rows.

Pennant stitch Work over a number of sts divisible by 6. *Row 1* *K1, P5*. *Row 2* *K4, P2*. *Row 3* *K3, P3*. *Row 4* *K2, P4*. *Row 5* *K5, P1*. *Row 6* As row 4. *Row 7* As row 3. *Row 8* As row 2. Rep these 8 rows.

Pinnacle crepe stitch Work over a number of sts divisible by 18 + 1. *Rows 1 and 3* P1, *(K2, P2) twice, K1, (P2, K2) twice, P1*. *Rows 2 and 4* K1, *(P2, K2) twice, P1, (K2, P2) twice, K1*. *Rows 5 and 7* P1, *P1, K2, P2, K2, P3, (K2, P2) twice*. *Rows 6 and 8* K1, *K1, P2, K2, P2, K3, (P2, K2) twice*. *Rows 9 and 11* As rows 2 and 4. *Rows 10 and 12* As rows 1 and 3. *Rows 13 and 15* As rows 6 and 8. *Rows 14 and 16* As rows 5 and 7. Rep these 16 rows.

Pyramid stitch Work over a number of sts divisible by 8 + 1. *Rows 1 and 3 (RS)* *P1, K1*, end with P1. *Rows 2 and 4* *K1, P1*, end with K1. *Rows 5 and 7* *P2, (K1, P1) 3 times*, end with P1. *Rows 6 and 8* *K2, (P1, K1) 3 times*, end with K1. *Rows 9 and 11* *P3, K1, P1, K1, P2*, end with P1. *Rows 10 and 12* *K3, P1, K1, P1, K2*, end with K1. *Rows 13 and 15* *P4, K1, P3*, end with P1. *Rows 14 and 16* *K4, P1, K3*, end with K1. Rep these 16 rows.

Dropped stitch patterns

Large honeycomb stitch   Bee stitch
Twin bee stitch   Diamond bee stitch

Large honeycomb stitch Work over a number of sts divisible by 2 + 1. *Row 1* K1, *P1, K1*. *Row 2* P1, *K1, P1*. *Row 3* K1, *P1, K1*. *Row 4* P1, *K1, P1*. *Row 5* *K1, work a bee (K into next st on left-hand needle 4 rows down, letting the st drop off left-hand needle and unravel)*, end with K1. *Row 6* As row 2. *Row 7* As row 1. *Row 8* As row 2. *Row 9* K1, P1, *work a bee, P1*, end with K1. *Row 10* Rep from row 2.

Bee stitch Work over a number of sts divisible by 6 + 5. *Row 1 and all odd rows (WS)* K. *Rows 2 and 4* P. *Row 6* *P5, work a bee (K into next st on left-hand needle 5 rows down, letting the st drop off the left-hand needle and unravel)*, rep from * to *, end with P5. *Rows 8 and 10* P. *Row 12* P2, *work a bee, P5*, end with P2. *Row 14* Rep from row 2.

Twin bee stitch Work over a number of sts divisible by 7 + 4. *Rows 1, 3, 5, 7 and 9* P. *Rows 2, 4, 6, 8 and 10* K. *Row 11* *P4, work a bee (K into next st on left-hand needle 4 rows down, letting the st drop off left-hand needle and unravel), P1, work a bee*, end with P4. *Row 12* Rep from row 2.

Diamond bee stitch Work over a number of sts divisible by 4 + 3. *Row 1 (RS)* P3, *K1, P3*. *Row 2* K. *Row 3* P. *Row 4* K3, *work a bee (K into next st on left-hand needle 3 rows down, letting st drop off left-hand needle and unravel), K3*. *Row 5* P1, *K1, P3*, end with K1, P1. *Row 6* K. *Row 7* P. *Row 8* K1, *work a bee, K3*, end with work a bee, K1. Rep these 8 rows.

Honeycomb stitch Work over an even number of sts. *Rows 1 and 3* K. *Row 2* *K1, K1d (K into next st, 1 row down)*. *Row 4* *K1d, K1*. Rep these 4 rows.

Dust stitch Work over an even number of sts. *Row 1* *P1, ybk, sl1 P yfwd*. *Row 2 and all even rows* P. *Row 3* *Ybk, sl1 P yfwd, P1*. *Row 5* Rep from row 1.

Sand stitch Work over an even number of sts. *Rows 1 and 2* K. *Row 3* *K1, K1d (K into next st, 1 row down)*. *Row 4* *With the right-hand needle lift the floating horizontal thread from K1d of previous row and K it tog with the st above it, K1*. *Row 5* *K1d, K1*. *Row 6* *K1, then work as for row 4*. *Row 7* Rep from row 3.

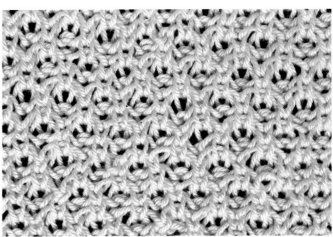

Alternating honeycomb stitch Work over an even number of sts. *Row 1* K. *Rows 2, 3, 4 and 5* *K1, K1d (K into next st, 1 row down)*, end with K2. *Rows 6, 7, 8 and 9* K2, *K1d, K1*. *Row 10* Rep from row 2.

Slipped stitch patterns

Slipped stocking stitch   Slipped granite stitch
Mock 1/1 rib   Tunisian rib

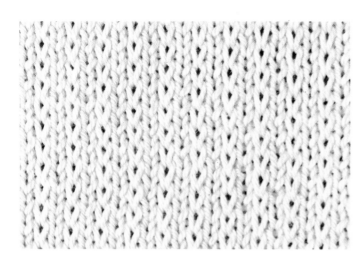

Slipped stocking stitch Work over an odd number of sts. *Row 1 (WS)* P. *Row 2* K1, *sl1 ybk, K1*. Rep these 2 rows.

Slipped granite stitch Work over a number of sts divisible by 4. *Row 1* *K2, sl2 P ybk*. *Row 2* *P2, K2*. *Row 3* *Sl2 P ybk, K2*. *Row 4* *K2, P2*. Rep these 4 rows.

Mock 1/1 rib This stitch is less elastic than rib as the slipped stitches prevent it from stretching. It may also be worked as a 2/2 version. Work over an odd number of sts. *Row 1 (WS)* K1, *P1, K1*. *Row 2* P1, *sl1 P yfwd, P1*. Rep these 2 rows.

Tunisian rib Work over an even number of sts. *Row 1 (RS)* K. *Row 2 and all even rows* *Sl1 P yfwd, yfwd, K1, making a st*, end with K1. *Row 3 and all odd rows* *K1, K2tog tbl (the sl st and made st of previous row)*. Rep last 2 rows.

Slipped stitch patterns
Stamen stitch   Slipped moss stitch
Garland stitch   3/1 stitch

Stamen stitch This is a firm horizontal stitch, giving a honey-comb effect, and can be worked on either large or small gauge needles. In this example large needles are used, so that the weave appears more open. Work over an even number of sts. *Row 1 and all odd rows* P. *Row 2 (RS)* *Sl1 P yfwd, P1*. *Row 4* *P1, sl1 P yfwd*. Rep from row 1.

Slipped moss stitch Work over an even number of sts. *Row 1* *K1, sl1 yfwd. *Row 2* *P1, sl1 ybk. *Row 3* As row 2. *Row 4* As row 1. Rep these 4 rows.

Garland stitch Work over an odd number of sts. *Row 1* K. *Row 2* P. *Row 3* *P1, sl1 P yfwd*. *Row 4* *P1, K sl st on previous row*, end with P1. Rep these 4 rows.

3/1 stitch Work over a number of sts divisible by 4 + 3. *Row 1 (RS)* K3, *sl1 ybk, K3*. *Row 2* K3, *sl1 yfwd, K3*. *Row 3* K1, *sl1 ybk, K3*, end with sl1, K1. *Row 4* K1, *sl1 P yfwd, K3*, end with sl1 P yfwd, K1. Rep these 4 rows.

Slipped stitch patterns

Link stitch   Zip stitch
Diagonal slip stitch   Mock 2/2 rib

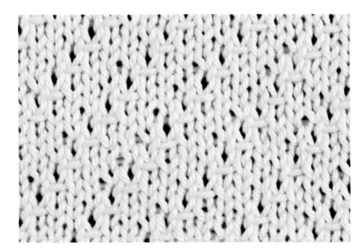

Link stitch Work over an odd number of sts. *Row 1* *K1, sl1 P yfwd*. *Row 2* P. Rep these 2 rows.

Zip stitch Work over a number of sts divisible by 3 + 1. *Row 1 (WS)* K. *Row 2* *K1, sl2 P yfwd*, end with K1. Rep these 2 rows.

Diagonal slip stitch Work over a number of sts divisible by 4. *Row 1* *K3, sl1 P yfwd*. *Row 2 and all even rows* P. *Row 3* *K2, sl1 P yfwd, K1*. *Row 5* *K1, sl1 P yfwd, K2*. *Row 7* *Sl1 P yfwd, K3*. *Row 9* Rep from row 1.

Mock 2/2 rib stitch This has the appearance of normal rib, but has only slight elasticity, as the slipped stitch prevents stretching. Work over a number of sts divisible by 4 + 2. *Row 1 (WS)* K2, *P2, K2*. *Row 2* P2, *sl2 P yfwd, P2*. Rep these 2 rows.

Diagonal cloth stitch Work over a number of sts divisible by 4 + 2. *Row 1* *K2, sl2 P yfwd*, end with K2. *Row 2 and all even rows* P. *Row 3* Sl1 P yfwd, *K2, sl2 P yfwd*, end with K1. *Row 5* Sl2 P yfwd, *K2, sl2 P yfwd*. *Row 7* K1, *sl2 P yfwd, K2*, end with sl1 P yfwd. *Row 8* P. Rep these 8 rows.

Zigzag stitch Work over a number of sts divisible by 4 + 1. *Row 1* P. *Row 2* K1, *sl1 P ybk, K3. *Row 3* *P3, sl1 P yfwd*, end with P1. *Row 4* K1, *drop sl st to front of work, K2, pick up sl st and K it, K1*. *Row 5* P. *Row 6* K5, *sl1 P ybk, K3*. *Row 7* *P3, sl1 P yfwd*, end with P5. *Row 8* K3, *sl2 P ybk, let sl st drop as above, sl same 2 sts to left-hand needle, pick up dropped st and K into it, K3*, end with K2. Rep these 8 rows.

Box stitch Work over a number of sts divisible by 12. *Rows 1, 3, 5, 7 and 9* *K9, sl3 P yfwd*. *Row 2 and all even rows* P. *Rows 11, 13 and 15* *K1, sl3 P yfwd*. *Row 17* Rep from row 1.

Slipped diamond stitch Work over a number of sts divisible by 16 + 2. (Slip all sts purlwise with yfwd.) *Row 1 and all odd rows (WS)* P. *Row 2* K1, *K3, sl2, K3, sl1, K3, sl2, K2*, end with K1. *Row 4* K1, *K2, sl2, K3, sl3, K3, sl2, K1*, end with K1. *Row 6* K1, *(K1, sl2, K3, sl2) twice*, end with K1. *Row 8* K1, sl2, *(K3, sl2) twice, K3, sl3*, end with sl1, K1. *Row 10* K1, *sl1, K3, sl2, K5, sl2, K3*, end with K1. *Row 12* As row 8. *Row 14* As row 6. *Row 16* As row 4. Rep these 16 rows.

Eyelet stitches

Parallel eyelet stitch   Triple eyelet stitch
Slipped eyelet stitch   Embroidered eyelet stitch

Parallel eyelet stitch   Work over a number of sts divisible by 7. *Row 1* *K2, P2tog, make 1, K3*. *Row 2 and all even rows* P. *Rows 3 and 7* K. *Row 5* *K3, make 1, P2tog, K2*. *Row 8* P. Rep these 8 rows.

Triple eyelet stitch   Work over a number of sts divisible by 8 + 7. *Row 1 and all odd rows (WS)* P. *Row 2* K. *Row 4* K2, make 1, sl1, K2tog, psso, make 1 *K5, make 1, sl1, K2tog, psso, make 1*, end with K2. *Row 6* K3, make 1, sl1, K1, psso, *K6, make 1, sl1, K1, psso*, end with K2. *Row 8* K. *Row 10* K1, *K5, make 1, sl1, K2tog, psso, make 1*, end with K6. *Row 12* K7, *make 1, sl1, K1, psso, K6*. Rep these 12 rows.

Slipped eyelet stitch   Work over a number of sts divisible by 4. *Row 1* K. *Row 2* *P4, make 1*. *Row 3* *Make 1, drop made st from previous row, sl1 K-wise, K3, pass sl st over last 3 sts*. *Row 4* P. Rep these 4 rows.

Embroidered eyelet stitch   Work over a number of sts divisible by 21 + 3. *Row 1 and all odd rows (WS)* P, working P1, K1 into any made sts of a previous row. *Row 2* K. *Row 4* K10, *K2tog, make 1, sl1, K1, psso, K17*, end with K10. *Row 6* K6, *K2tog, make 1, sl1, K1, psso, K4, K2tog, make 1, sl1, K1, psso, K9*, end with K6. *Row 8* K3, *K2tog, make 1, sl1, K1, psso, K3*. *Row 10* As row 6. *Row 12* As row 4. Rep these 12 rows.

Polka eyelet stitch Work over an even number of sts. *Row 1 (RS)* K. *Row 2* P. *Row 3* P1, *yrn, P2tog*, P1. *Row 4* P. *Rows 5 and 6* As rows 1 and 2. *Row 7* P2, *yrn, P2tog*. *Row 8* As row 4. Rep these 8 rows.

Eyelet insertion stitch Work over an odd number of sts. *Row 1 (RS)* K. *Row 2* P. *Rows 3 and 4* K. *Row 5* *K2tog, make 1*, end with K1. *Row 6* K. Rep these 6 rows.

Eyelet rib Work over a number of sts divisible by 6 + 2. *Row 1* *P2, K2tog, make 2, sl1, K1, psso*, end with P2. *Row 2* K2, *P1, work (K1, P1) into made sts of previous row, P1, K2*. *Row 3* *P2, K4*, end with P2. *Row 4* P2, *K4, P2*. Rep these 4 rows.

Fishbone stitch Work over a number of sts divisible by 9. *Row 1* *(K2tog, make 1) twice, K1, (make 1, K2tog tbl) twice*. *Row 2* P. Rep these 2 rows.

Eyelet stitches

Purled calyx stitch	Eyelet trellis
Peacock stitch	Lace eyelet stitch

Purled calyx stitch Work over a number of sts divisible by 5 + 3. *Row 1* K3, *P2, K3*. *Row 2* *P3, K1, make 1, K1*, end with P3. *Row 3* K3, *P1, K1, P1, K3*. *Row 4* *P3tog, K1, make 1, K1, make 1, K1*, end with P3tog. *Row 5* Work (K1, make 1, K1) into next st, *P1, P3tog, P1, work (K1, make 1, K1) into next st. *Row 6* *P3, ybk, sl1, K1 tbl but do not drop st from needle, lift sl st over loop on right needle, K2tog loop on left-hand needle with next st*, end with P3. Rep these 6 rows.

Eyelet trellis Work over a number of sts divisible by 8. *Rows 1 and 5* P. *Row 2* *(K2tog) twice, make 2, (sl1, K1, psso) twice*. *Row 3* *P2tog tbl into made sts, work (P1, K1) 3 times, P2tog*. *Row 4* K1, *K6, K2tog without letting sts drop, K first st again and let both drop from the needle*, end with K7. *Row 6* K4, *(K2tog) twice, make 2, (sl1, K1, psso) twice*, end with K4. *Row 7* P4, rep from * to *, as in row 3, P4. *Row 8* K3, *K2tog, K again into first st as in row 4, K6*, end with K3. Rep these 8 rows.

Peacock stitch Work over number of sts divisible by 18. *Row 1 (RS)* K. *Row 2* P. *Row 3* (K2tog) 3 times, (make 1, K1) 6 times, (K2tog) 3 times*. *Row 4* K. Rep these 4 rows.

Lace eyelet stitch Both sides of work look the same. Work over a number of sts divisible by 4 + 4 for the selvedge. (N.B. The 3rd row should be worked loosely, using a needle 3 or 4 sizes larger than for the rest of the work.) *Row 1* P2, *make 1, P4tog*, end with P2. *Row 2* K2, *K1, (K1, P1, K1) into st made on previous row*, end with K2. *Row 3* K. Rep these 3 rows.

Zigzag eyelet stitch Work over a number of sts divisible by 11 + 2. *Row 1 (WS) and all odd rows* P. *Row 2* K6, *make 1, sl1, K1, psso, K9*, end with K5. *Row 4* K7, *make 1, sl1, K1, psso, K9*, end with K4. *Row 6* K3, *K2tog, make 1, K3, make 1, sl1, K1, psso, K4*, end with K3. *Row 8* *K2, K2tog, make 1, K5, make 1, sl1, K1, psso*, end with K2. *Row 10* K1, *K2tog, make 1, K7, make 1, sl1, K1, psso*, end with K1. *Row 12* *K2tog, make 1, K9*, end with K2. Rep these 12 rows.

Divided lozenge stitch Work over a number of sts divisible by 10 + 6. *Row 1* K1, make 1, *K3, sl2 K-wise, K1, p2sso, K3, make 1, K1, make 1*, end with K3, sl1, K1, psso. *Row 2 and all even rows* P. *Row 3* K2, make 1, *K2, sl2 K-wise, K1, p2sso, K2, make 1, K3, make 1*, end with K2, sl1, K1, psso. *Row 5* K3, make 1, *K1, sl2 K-wise, K1, p2sso, K1, make 1, K5, make 1*, end with make 1, K1, sl1, K1, psso. *Row 7* K4, make 1, *sl2, K1, p2sso, make 1, K7, make 1*, end with sl1, K1, psso. *Row 9* Sl1, K1, psso, K3, make 1, *K1, make 1, K3, sl2 K-wise, K1, p2sso, K3, make 1*, end with K1. *Row 11* Sl1, K1, psso, K2, make 1 *K3, make 1, K2, sl2 K-wise, K1, p2sso, K2, make 1*, end with K2. *Row 13* Sl1, K1, psso, K1, make 1, *K5, make 1, K1, sl2 K-wise, K1, p2sso, K1, make 1*, end with K3. *Row 15* Sl1, K1, psso, make 1, *K7, make 1, K1, sl2 K-wise, K1, p2sso, make 1*, end with K4. *Row 16* P. Rep these 16 rows.

Tadpole stitch Work over a number of sts divisible by 6 + 1. *Rows 1, 3, and 5* K1, *make 1, sl2 K-wise, K1, p2sso, make 1, K3*. *Row 2 and all even rows* P. *Rows 7, 9 and 11* K1, *K3, make 1, sl2 K-wise, K1, p2sso, make 1*, end with sl1, K1, psso, K1. *Row 13* Rep from row 1.

'V' panel stitch Work over a number of sts divisible by 12. *Row 1* *K3, make 1, sl1, K1, psso, K2, K2tog, make 1, K1, make 1, psso*. *Row 2 and all even rows* P. *Row 3* *K1, K2tog, make 1, K1, make 1, sl1, K1, psso, K1, K2tog, make 1, K1, make 1, sl1, K1, psso*. *Row 5* *K2tog, make 1, K3, make 1, sl1, K1, psso, K2tog, make 1, K1, make 1, sl1, K1, psso*. *Row 6* P. Rep these 6 rows.

Eyelet stitches
Bunches of roses   Peacock's tail pattern
Swallow eyelet pattern   Shetland eyelet pattern

Bunches of roses Work over a number of sts divisible by 16 + 9. *Row 1 and all odd rows* P. *Row 2* K10, *K2tog, make 1, K1, make 1, sl1, K1, psso, K11*, end with K10. *Row 4* K9, *K2tog, make 1, K3, make 1, sl1, K1, psso, K9*. *Row 6* K10, *make 1, sl1, K1, psso, make 1, K3tog, make 1, K11*, end with K10. *Row 8* K11, *make 1, sl1, K2tog, psso, make 1, K13*, end with K11. *Row 10* K2, *K2tog, make 1, K1, make 1, sl1, K1, psso, K11*, end with K2. *Row 12* K1, rep from * to * as in row 4, and end with K1. *Row 14* K2, rep from * to * as in row 6, and end with K2. *Row 16* K3, *make 1, sl1, K2tog, psso, make 1, K13*, end with K3. Rep these 16 rows.

Peacock's tail pattern Work over 28 sts. *Rows 1 and 3 (RS)* K. *Rows 2 and 4* P. *Row 5* K12, K2tog, yrn twice, sl1, K1, psso, K12. *Row 6 and all even rows (WS)* P to end, working P1, K1 into 2 made sts of previous row if necessary. *Rows 7, 11, 15, 19, 23 and 27* K. *Row 9* K10 (K2tog, yrn twice, sl1, K1, psso) twice, K10. *Row 13* K8, (K2tog, yrn twice, sl1, K1, psso) 3 times, K8. *Row 17* K6, (K2tog, yrn twice, sl1, K1, psso) 4 times, K6. *Row 21* K4 (K2tog, yrn twice, sl1, K1, psso) 5 times, K4. *Row 25* K2 (K2tog, yrn twice, sl1, K1, psso) 6 times, K2. *Row 29* As row 13. *Row 30* As row 6. Rep these 30 rows.

Swallow eyelet pattern The eyelet pattern is worked over 9 sts and is spaced with 1 or more sts in st st. In the sample the spacing is 6 sts. *Row 1* *K4, make 1, sl1, K1, psso, K3*. *Row 2 and all even rows* P. *Row 3* *K2, K2tog, make 1, K1, make 1, sl1, K1, psso, K2. *Row 5* *K1, K2tog, make 1, K3, make 1, sl1, K1, psso, K1*. *Row 7* *K2tog, make 1, K5, make 1, sl1, K1, psso*. *Row 8* P. Rep these 8 rows.

Shetland eyelet pattern Work over 9 sts. *Row 1 and all odd rows (WS)* P. *Row 2* K2, K2tog, make 1, K1, make 1, sl1, K1, psso, K2. *Row 4* K1, K2tog, make 1, K3, make 1, sl1, K1, psso, K1. *Row 6* K1, make 1, sl1, K1, psso, make 1, sl2, K1, p2sso, make 1, K2tog, make 1, K1. *Row 8* K3, make 1, sl2, K1, p2sso, make 1, K3. Rep these 8 rows.

Raised leaf pattern Work over a number of sts divisible by 7 + 6. *Row 1* P6, *make 1, K1, make 1, P6*. *Rows 2 and 14* *K6, P3*, K6. *Row 3* P6, *K1, make 1, K1, make 1, K1, P6*. *Rows 4 and 12* *K6, P5*, K6. *Row 5* P6, *K2, make 1, K1, make 1, K2, P6*. *Rows 6 and 10* *K6, P7*, K6. *Row 7* P6, *K3, make 1, K1, make 1, K3, P6*. *Row 8* *K6, P9*, K6. *Row 9* P6, *sl1, K1, psso, K5, K2tog, P6*. *Row 11* P6, *sl1, K1, psso, K3, K2tog, P6*. *Row 13* P6, *sl1, K1, psso, K1, K2tog, P6*. *Row 15* K6, *sl1, K2tog, psso, K6*. *Rows 16, 18 and 20* K. *Rows 17 and 19* P.

Eyelet fantasy stitch Work over a number of sts divisible by 13. *Row 1* *K4, K2tog, make 1, K1, make 1, sl1, K1, psso, K4*. *Row 2 and all even rows* P. *Row 3* *K3, K2tog, K1, make 1, K1, make 1, K1, sl1, K1, psso, K3*. *Row 5* *K2, K2tog, K2, make 1, K1, make 1, K2, sl1, K1, psso, K2*. *Row 7* *K1, K2tog, K3, make 1, K1, make 1, K3, sl1, K1, psso, K1*. *Row 9* *K1, make 1, K2tog, K7, sl1, K1, psso, make 1, K1*. *Row 11* *K2, make 1, sl1, K1, psso, K5, K2tog, make 1, K2*. *Row 13* *K3, make 1, sl1, K1, psso, K3, K2tog, make 1, K3*. *Row 15* *K4, make 1, sl1, K1, psso, K1, K2tog, make 1, K4*. *Row 17* *K5, make 1, sl1, K2tog, psso, make 1, K5*. *Row 19* Rep from row 1.

Candelabra stitch Work over a number of sts divisible by 8 + 1. *Row 1* *K1, make 1, K2, sl1, K2tog, psso, K2, make 1*, end with K1. *Row 2 and all even rows* P. *Rows 3, 5 and 7* As row 1. *Row 9* K2, *K2tog, make 1, K1, make 1, sl1, K1, psso, K3*, end with K2. *Row 11* *K1, K2tog, make 1, K3, make 1, sl1, K1, psso*, end with K1. *Row 13* K2tog, *make 1, K5, make 1, sl2, K1, p2sso*, end with sl1, K1, psso. *Row 15* Rep from row 1.

Eyelet pyramids Work over a number of sts divisible by 11 + 5. *Row 1* *K3, (make 1, sl1, K1, psso) 4 times*, end with K5. *Row 2 and all even rows* P. *Row 3* *K4, (make 1, sl1, K1, psso) 3 times, K1*, end with K5. *Row 5* *K5, (make 1, sl1, K1, psso) twice, K2*, end with K5. *Row 7* *K6, make 1, sl1, K1, psso, K3*, end with K5. *Row 9* K5, rep from * to * as row 1. *Row 11* K5, rep from * to * as row 3. *Row 13* K5, rep from * to * as row 5. *Row 15* K5, rep from * to * as row 7. *Row 16* P. Rep these 16 rows.

Lace stitches

Lace stitch   Turkish stitch   Fantasy lace stitch
Lace rib stitch   Lace stocking stitch   Undulating lace stitch

Lace stitch Work over an even number of sts. *Row 1 and all following rows* K1, *make 1, sl1, K1, psso*, end with K1.

Turkish stitch Work over an even number of sts. *Row 1 and all following rows* K1, *make 1, K2tog*, end with K1.

Fantasy lace stitch Work over a number of sts divisible by 4. *Row 1 and all following rows* *K1, make 1, P2tog, K1*.

Lace rib stitch Work over a number of sts divisible by 3. *Row 1 and all following rows* *K1, make 1, K2tog*.

Lace stocking stitch Work over a number of sts divisible by 3. *Row 1 (RS)* *K1, make 2, K2tog*. *Row 2* P to end, working the first made st and dropping the second. Rep these 2 rows.

Undulating lace stitch Work over a number of sts divisible by 3. *Row 1 (RS)* *K1, make 2, K2tog*. *Row 2* P to end, working the first made st and dropping the second. *Row 3* *K2tog, make 2, K1*. *Row 4* As row 2. Rep these 4 rows.

Loop stitch: 1st method 1. This method results in rows of looped fringing and over many rows a fluffy, fur-like effect is achieved. Use a soft yarn. *Rows 1, 2, 3 and 4 K. Row 5 (WS)* *Lift the yarn at the back of the work with the left index finger.

2. K into the first st, making a loop and without letting the stitch drop.

3. With the right-hand needle transfer the loop to the left-hand needle, so making two stitches, still holding the yarn on the left index finger.

4. K2tog tbl, withdraw the finger from the loop ready to make another on the following stitch*. Rep from * to * in each stitch. *Row 6* K tbl to end. Rep these 6 rows.

2nd method 1. This requires a heavier yarn, and results in long wide loops. Work over an even number of sts. *Rows 1 and 2 K. Row 3* K1, *wind the yarn two or three times round the left index finger.

2. Pass the right-hand needle into the following stitch and the loops on the finger.

3. Using the right-hand needle, draw the loops on the finger through the stitch on the left-hand needle.

4. K into next stitch, pulling it tight*. Rep from * to * on next two stitches, and so on to the end of the row, ending K1.

5. *Row 4* K, working the two loops as K2tog tbl. *Rows 5 to 8* K. Start again at row 3. The number of rows between the looped rows can be varied according to the effect required.

Fancy stitches

Rope stitch
Undulating rib
Crossed thorn stitch

Zigzag columns
Crossed lacing stitch
Crossed thorn ribbing

Rope stitch Work over a number of sts divisible by 6 + 4. *Row 1* P4, *K2, P4*. *Row 2* *K4, PC2R (P second st, then P first st)*, end with K4. Rep these 2 rows.

Zigzag columns Work over a number of sts divisible by 8 + 2. *Row 1 (WS)* K1, *K7, P1*, end with K1. *Row 2* P1, *C2L, P6*, end with P1. *Row 3* K1, *K6, P1, K1*, end with K1. *Row 4* P1, *P1, C2L, P5*, end with P1. *Rows 5 to 8* Rep these 4 rows. *Rows 9 to 16* Rep rows 1 to 8 working C2R instead of C2L.

Undulating rib Work over a number of sts divisible by 9 + 5. *Row 1* *P5, C2R, C2L*, end with P5. *Row 2* Work sts as set. *Row 3* *P5, C2L, C2R*, end with P5. *Row 4* As row 2. Rep these 4 rows.

Crossed lacing stitch Work over a number of sts divisible by 4. *Row 1 (RS)* K1, *C2L, K2*, end with K1. *Row 2* K1, *P into second st, then P into first st, slipping both from needle tog, K2*, end with K1. Rep these 2 rows.

Crossed thorn stitch Work over a number of sts divisible by 4. *Row 1* *C2R, C2L*. *Row 2* P. Rep these 2 rows.

Crossed thorn ribbing Work over a number of sts divisible by 12 + 4. *Row 1* *K4, (C2R, C2L) twice*, end with K4. *Row 2* P. Rep these 2 rows.

Fancy stitches

Diagonal crossed stitch   Crossed purl stitch
Crater stitch   Crossed granite stitch
Zigzag rib   Wave stitch

Diagonal crossed stitch Work over an even number of sts. *Rows 1 and 3 (WS)* P. *Row 2* *K2tog without letting sts drop from needle, and K into first st again, letting both sts drop from needle*. *Row 4* K1, rep 2nd row from * to *, end with K1. Rep these 4 rows.

Crossed purl stitch Work over an even number of sts. *Rows 1 and 3* K. *Row 2 (WS)* *P2tog without letting sts drop, P again into first st letting both sts drop off needle*. *Row 4* P1, rep 2nd row from * to *, end with P1. Rep these 4 rows.

Crater stitch Work over a number of sts divisible by 8 + 1. *Row 1* K. *Row 2 and all even rows* P. *Row 3* K1, *C2R, C2L, K4*. *Row 5* K1, *C2L, C2R, K4*. *Row 7* K. *Row 9* K5, *C2R, C2L, K4*, end C2R, C2L. *Row 11* K5, *C2L, C2R, K4*, end with C2L, C2R. *Row 12* P. Rep these 12 rows.

Crossed granite stitch Work over a number of sts divisible by 8 + 2. *Row 1* *K2, (C2R) 3 times*, end with K2. *Row 2* P. *Row 3* *K2, (K into third st on left-hand needle, then into second, then into first and let the 3 sts drop off needle tog) twice*, end with K2. *Row 4* P. Rep these 4 rows.

Zigzag rib Work over a number of sts divisible by 6. *Row 1* *P2, (T2R) twice*. *Row 2* *(T2L) twice, K2*. Rep these 2 rows.

Wave stitch Work over a number of sts divisible by 4 + 2. *Row 1* P2, *P3, K1*. *Row 2 and all even rows* Work the sts as set. *Row 3* P2, *K fourth st on left-hand needle, P into each of the 3 P sts, letting 4 sts drop tog*. *Row 5* P2, *K1, P3*. *Row 7* P2, *sl next st onto cable needle and hold at front of work, P3, then K1 from cable needle*. *Row 8* As row 2. Rep these 8 rows.

Fancy stitches

Acorn stitch   Bow stitch
Pebble stitch   Peppercorn stitch

Acorn stitch Work over a number of sts divisible by 4 + 3. *Rows 1 to 4* Work in st st. *Row 5* P3, *(K1, P1, K1) all in next st, P3*. *Row 6* K3, *P3, K3*. *Row 7* P3, *K3, P3*. *Rows 8 and 9* As rows 6 and 7. *Row 10* P5, *K3tog, P3*. Rep these 10 rows.

Bow stitch Work over a number of sts divisible by 18 + 9. *Rows 1 and 7 (RS)* K9, *P9, K9*. *Rows 2 and 8* P9, *K9, P9*. *Rows 3, 5, 13 and 15* K. *Rows 4, 6, 10, 14, 16 and 20* P. *Row 9* K13, *insert right-hand needle into the front of the next st, 9 rows down, draw through a loop and sl it onto left-hand needle and K it tog with first st on needle, K17*, end with K13. *Rows 11 and 17* P9, *K9, P9*. *Rows 12 and 18* K9, *P9, K9*. *Row 19* K4, *draw through a loop from the 9th row down and K it tog with first st on left-hand needle, as in row 9, K17*, end with K4. Rep these 20 rows.

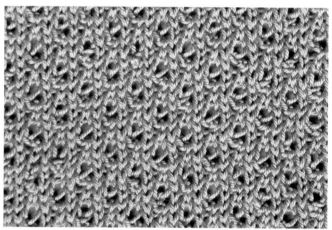

Pebble stitch Work over a number of sts divisible by 4. *Row 1 (RS)* P. *Row 2* K2, *work (K1, P1, K1) into next st, P3tog*, end with K2. *Row 3* P. *Row 4* K2, *P3tog, work (K1, P1, K1) into next st*, end with K2. Rep these 4 rows.

Peppercorn stitch Work over a number of sts divisible by 4 + 3. *Rows 1 and 3 (WS)* P. *Row 2* K3, *(K next st and sl back on left-hand needle) 3 times, K st again, called wk4, K3*. *Row 4* K1*, wk4, K3*, end with K1. Rep these 4 rows.

44

Elongated rhombus stitch Work over a number of sts divisible by 12 + 1. *Row 1 (WS)* P2, *K4, P1, K4, P3*, end with K4, P1, K4, P2. *Row 2* K1, *T2L, P3, K1, P3, T2R, K1*. *Row 3* P1, *K1, P1, (K3, P1) twice, K1, P1*. *Row 4* K1, *P1, T2L, P2, K1, P2, T2R, P1, K1*. *Row 5* P1, *K2, P1*. *Row 6* K1, *P2, T2L, P1, K1, P1, T2R, P2, K1*. *Row 7* P1, *K3, (P1, K1) twice, P1, K3, P1*. *Row 8* K1, *P3, T2L, K1, T2R, P3, K1*. *Rows 9 and 11* P1, *K4, P3, K4, P1*. *Row 10* K1, *P4, ytf, sl next 3 sts onto right-hand needle, ybk, sl same 3 sts onto left-hand needle, ytf, sl 3 sts onto right-hand needle – called wrap 3, P4, K1*. *Row 12* K1, *P3, T2R, K1, T2L, P3, K1*. *Rows 13, 15, 17 and 19* As rows 7, 5, 3 and 1. *Row 14* K1, *P2, T2R, P1, K1, P1, T2L, P2, K1*. *Row 16* K1, *P1, T2R, P2, K1, P2, T2L, P1, K1*. *Row 18* K1, *T2R, P3, K1, P3, T2L, K1*. *Row 20* K2, *P4, K1, P4, wrap 3*, end with P4, K1, P4, K2. Rep these 20 rows.

Vertical zigzag stitch Work over a number of sts divisible by 9. *Row 1* *K3, (T2R) 3 times*. *Row 2 and every alt row* P to end. *Row 3* *K2, (T2R) 3 times, K1*. *Row 5* *K1, (T2R) 3 times, K2*. *Row 7* *(T2R) 3 times, K3*. *Row 9* *(T2L) 3 times, K3*. *Row 11* *K1, (T2L) 3 times, K2*. *Row 13* *K2, (T2L) 3 times, K1*. *Row 15* *K3, (T2L) 3 times*. *Row 17* Rep from row 1.

Purled rhombus stitch Work over a number of sts divisible by 8. *Row 1* *K2, C2R, C2L, K2*. *Row 2* *K2, sl1 P yfwd, P2, sl1 P yfwd, K2*. *Row 3* *K1, C2R, K2, C2L, K1*. *Row 4* *K1, sl1 P yfwd, P4, sl1 P yfwd, K1*. *Row 5* *C2R, K4, C2L*. *Row 6* *Sl1 P yfwd, P6, sl1 P yfwd*. *Row 7* K. *Row 8* As row 6. *Rows 9 to 13* As rows 5 to 1, reading C2L for C2R and vice versa. *Rows 14 and 16* *K3, sl2 P yfwd, K3*. *Row 15* K. *Row 17* Rep from row 1.

Sycamore stitch Work over a number of sts divisible by 8. *Row 1* *C2L, K6*. *Row 2* *P6, sl1 P yfwd, K1*. *Row 3* *K1, C2L, K5*. *Row 4* *P5, sl1 P yfwd, K2*. *Row 5* *K2, C2L, K4*. *Row 6* P4, sl1 P yfwd, K3*. *Row 7* K. *Row 8* P. *Row 9* *K6, C2R*. *Row 10* *K1, sl1 P yfwd, P6*. *Row 11* *K5, C2R, K1*. *Row 12* *K2, sl1 P yfwd, P5*. *Row 13* *K4, C2R, K2*. *Row 14* *K3, sl1 P yfwd, P4*. *Row 15* K. *Row 16* P. *Row 17* Rep from row 1.

Popcorn Work over a number of sts divisible by 6 + 5. *Rows 1 to 4* K. *Row 5* K5, *work (K1, P1, K1, P1) all into next st, K5*. *Row 6* K5, *ytf, sl3, K1, sl third, second and first sts separately over the last st worked, completing the 'popcorn', K5*. *Rows 7 to 10* K. *Row 11* K2, *(K1, P1, K1, P1) all into next st, K5*, end with K2. *Row 12* K2, *ytf, sl3, K1, complete the 'popcorn' as in row 6, K5*, end with K2. Rep these 12 rows.

Alternating bobbles Work over a number of sts divisible by 6 + 5. *Rows 1 to 5* K. *Row 6* K5, *(make 1 and K1) 3 times into next st to make 6 sts for the bobble, turn the work, sl1, P5, turn the work again and sl1, K5, turn the work again and (P2tog) 3 times, turn again and complete the bobble with sl1, K2tog, psso, K5*. *Row 7* K5, *P1 tbl, K5*. *Rows 8 to 11* K. *Row 12* K8, *wk a bobble as in row 6, K5*, end with K3. *Row 13* K8, *P1 tbl, K5*, end with K3. Rep rows 2 to 13. If a larger bobble is required, turn the work twice more on the 6 sts.

Hazelnut stitch Work over a number of sts divisible by 6 + 2. *Row 1* *P2, K1*, end with P2. *Row 2* *K2, P1, K2 (K1, P1, K1, P1) all in next st*, end with K2. *Row 3* *P8, K1*, end with P2. *Row 4* K2, *P1, K8*. *Row 5* As row 3. *Row 6* K2, *P1, P4tog, P1*. *Row 7* As row 1. *Row 8* *K2, (K1, P1, K1, P1) all in next st, K2, P1*, end with K2. *Row 9* P2, *K1, P8*. *Row 10* *K8, P1*, end with K2. *Row 11* As row 9. *Row 12* K2*, P1, P4tog, P1*. Rep these 12 rows.

Pineapple stitch Work over a number of sts divisible by 6 + 2. *Row 1 (RS)* K1, *sl3 ybk, K2tog, pass the 3 slipped sts over, one at a time, loosely P (into the back, then into the front) twice and then into the back again of next st*, end with K1. *Row 2* P1, *K5, P1*, end with P1. *Rows 3 and 5* K1, *K1, P5*, end with K1. *Rows 4 and 6* As row 2. *Row 7* K1, *loosely P (into the back, then into the front) twice and then into the back again of next st, sl3 ybk, K2tog, pass the 3 slipped sts over one at a time*, end with K1. *Row 8* P1, *P1, K5*, end with P1. *Rows 9 and 11* K1, *P5, K1*, end with K1. *Rows 10 and 12* As row 8. Rep these 12 rows.

Shutter stitch Work over a number of sts divisible by 4. *Row 1* *Make 1, K4*. *Row 2* P. *Row 3* *Make 1, K into the third st on left-hand needle, then knit the second and first tog, C2L*. Rep rows 2 to 3.

Crossed link stitch Work over a number of sts divisible by 4. *Rows 1 and 3 (RS)* K1, *P2, K2*, end with P2, K1. *Row 2* P1, K1, *miss the next 3 sts, insert needle into fourth st and pull through a loop, then K first st on left-hand needle, P next 2 sts, drop the fourth (the st from which the loop was drawn)*, end with K1, P1. *Row 4* P1, *K2, P2*, end with K2, P1. Rep these 4 rows.

Crossed square stitch Work over a number of sts divisible by 18 + 10. *Rows 1, 3, 5, 7 and 9 (RS)* *(P1, C2R) 3 times, P1, K8 tbl*, end with (P1, C2R) 3 times, P1. *Rows 2, 4, 6, 8 and 10* *(K1, P2) 3 times, K1, P8 tbl*, end with (K1, P2) 3 times, K1. *Rows 11, 13, 15, 17 and 18* P1, *K8 tbl, (P1, C2R) 3 times, P1*, end with K8 tbl, P1. *Rows 12, 14, 16, 19 and 20* K1, *P8 tbl, (K1, P2) 3 times, K1*, end with P8 tbl, K1. Rep these 20 rows.

Brick stitch Work over a number of sts divisible by 14 + 4. *Rows 1 and 2* P. *Rows 3, 5 and 7* *K1, PC2R, K1, P10*, end with K1, PC2R, K1. *Rows 4, 6 and 8* *P1, K2, P1, K10*, end with P1, K2, P1. *Rows 9 and 10* P. *Rows 11, 13 and 15* *P7, K1, PC2R, K1, P3*, end with P4. *Rows 12, 14 and 16* *K7, P1, K2, P1, K3*, end with K4. Rep these 16 rows.

Working cables
Simple cable from right to left
Simple cable from left to right
Double cable with two cable needles

Simple cable from right to left 1. The number of stitches in the cable must be even. Work to the cable position, then put the first group of stitches to be cabled (the first 3 of a cable of 6 stitches) on a cable needle and hold at the front of the work.

2. Knit the following 3 stitches, then return to the cable needle and knit the stitches from it. When working the first stitch from the cable needle, take care that the yarn is pulled firmly to avoid a loose stitch at the back of the work.

Simple cable from left to right Put the first group of stitches to be cabled on the cable needle and hold at the back of the work. Work the following 3 stitches, then return to the cable needle and knit the stitches from it.

Double cable with two cable needles Work on 9 stitches. Put the first 3 stitches on a cable needle and hold at the back of the work. Then put the following 3 stitches on a cable needle and hold at the front of the work. Knit the following 3 stitches, then work the stitches from the cable needle at the back of the work and then from the cable needle at the front of the work. The result is a double cable crossed at the centre.

Simple cable For a 4 st cable moving to left (or to right) every 4 rows. *Rows 1 and 3 (WS)* *K2, P4*, end with K2. *Row 2* P2, *K4, P2*. *Row 4* *P2, put next 2 sts on cable needle to the front (or back), K2, K2 from cable needle*, end with P2. Rep these 4 rows. For a 6 st cable moving to left (or to right) every 6 rows: *Rows 1, 3, 5* *K2, P6*, end with K2. *Rows 2 and 4* *P2, K6*, end with P2. *Row 6* *P2, put next 3 sts on cable needle to the front (or back), K3, K3 from cable needle*, end with P2. Rep these 6 rows.

Ear of grain cable This sample shows a cable of 13 sts on a background of reverse st st. *Row 1 (RS)* K13. *Row 2* P13. *Row 3* Put 3 sts on cable needle, and hold at back of work, K3, K3 from cable needle, K1, put 3 sts on cable needle, and hold at front of work, K3, K3 from cable needle. *Row 4* P13. Rep these 4 rows.

Triple cable This cable is worked over 9 sts. This sample shows 3 sts reverse st st between each cable. *Rows 1 and 3 (WS)* *K3, P9*, end with K3. *Row 2* P3, *K9, P3*. *Row 4* *P3, put 3 sts on cable needle and hold at front of work, K3, K3 from cable needle, K3*, end with P3. *Rows 5 and 7* As rows 1 and 3. *Row 6* As row 2. *Row 8* *P3, K3, put 3 sts on cable needle and hold at back of work, K3, K3 from cable needle*, end with P3. Rep these 8 rows.

Composite cable This 18 st cable can be worked on a background of garter stitch or flanked by 5 sts reverse st st, as in this example. *Rows 1, 5 and 9* *P5, K18*, end with P5. *Row 2 and all even rows* Work the sts as set. *Row 3* *P5, (put 3 sts on cable needle and hold at back of work, K3, K3 from cable needle) 3 times*, end with P5. *Row 7* *P5, K3, (put 3 sts on cable needle and hold at front of work, K3, K3 from cable needle) twice, K3*, end with P5. *Row 11* Rep from row 3.

Cable patterns

Cross banded cable   Slanting cable
Wind on the sand   Twisted cable

Cross banded cable   This is a 10 st cable. This sample shows it on a reverse st st background. *Row 1* Make a left cross thus: place 2 sts on cable needle and hold at front of work, K2, K2 from cable needle, K5. *Row 2* P6, sl2 P-wise, P2. *Row 3* K2, make a left cross as above, K4. *Row 4* P4, sl2 P-wise, P4. *Row 5* K4, make a left cross as above, K2. *Row 6* P2, sl2 P-wise, P6. *Row 7* K6, make a cross as above. *Row 8* P10. Rep these 8 rows.

Slanting cable   Work over a number of sts divisible by 12 + 6. *Rows 1 and 3* *P6, K6*, end with P6. *Row 2 and all even rows* Work the sts as set. *Row 5* As for row 1, shifting the patt 1 st to the right; start, therefore, with P5, *K6, P6*, end with K1. *Row 7* Work the sts as set, and work a cable. *Row 9* Shift the patt again 1 st to the right and start with P4. Continue in this way, shifting the patt every 4 rows; *at the same time,* work a cable on 7th and every foll 6th row, working on 6 sts in st st. Place 3 sts on cable needle and hold at front of work, K3, K3 from cable needle.

Wind on the sand   Work over a number of sts divisible by 12. *Row 1* K. *Row 2 and all even rows* P. *Row 3* *Place 3 sts on cable needle and hold at front of work, K3, K3 from cable needle, K6*. *Row 5* K. *Row 7* *K6, place 3 sts on cable needle and hold at back of work, K3, K3 from cable needle*. *Row 8* P. *Row 9* Rep from row 3.

Twisted cable   Work over a number of sts divisible by 9 + 3. *Row 1* *P3, K6*, end with P3. *Row 2 and all even rows* Work sts as set. *Row 3* *P3, place 2 sts on cable needle and hold at back of work, K2, K2 from cable needle, K2*, end with P3. *Row 5* *P3, K2, place 2 sts on cable needle and hold at front of work, K2, K2 from cable needle*, end with P3. *Row 7* Rep from row 3.

Open cable This needs 2 cable needles. Work over a number of sts divisible by 16. *Row 1* *P2, K2*. *Rows 2 to 6* Work the sts as set. *Row 7* *P2, (work the first cable over next 6 sts), place 2 K sts on cable needle and hold at front of work, place 2 P sts on second cable needle and hold at back of work, K2, P2 from cable needle, K2 from cable needle, P2, K2, P2, K2*. *Rows 8 to 12* Work as rows 2 to 6. *Row 13* Shifting the cable in the foll way: *P2, K2, P2, K2, P2, work the cable on the 6 foll sts*. *Row 14* Rep from row 2.

Medallion cable Work over a number of sts divisible by 10 + 2. *Row 1* P2, *K8, P2*. *Row 2* K2, *P8, K2*. *Row 3* P2, *C4B, C4F, P2*. *Row 4* As row 2. *Rows 5 to 8* Rep rows 1 and 2 twice. *Row 9* P2, *C4F, C4B, P2*. *Row 10* As row 2. *Rows 11 and 12* As rows 1 and 2. Rep these 12 rows.

Simple chalice stitch Work over a number of sts divisible by 4 + 2. *Rows 1, 3 and 5* P2, *K2, P2*. *Rows 2 and 4* K2, *P2, K2*. *Row 6* K1, *place 1 st on cable needle and hold at front of work, P1, miss 1, K into next st, sl it over missed st, K1 from cable needle, P missed st*, end with K1. *Rows 7, 9 and 11* K2, *P2, K2*. *Rows 8 and 10* P2, *K2, P2*. *Row 12* K1, miss 1, K into next st, sl it over missed st as before, P missed st, rep from * to * as in row 6, and end with place 1 st on cable needle and hold front of work, P1, K1 from cable needle, K1. Rep these 12 rows.

Double chalice stitch Work over a number of sts divisible by 8 + 2. *Rows 1, 3, 5 and 7 (WS)* K2, *P2, K2*. *Rows 2, 4 and 6* P2, *K2, P2*. *Row 8* P2, *place 4 sts on cable needle and hold at back of work, K2, sl 2 P sts from cable needle onto left-hand needle and P them, K2 rem sts from cable needle, P2*. *Rows 9 to 15* As for rows 1 to 7. *Row 16* P2, K2, *P2, place next 4 sts on cable needle and hold at front of work, K2, sl 2 P sts from cable needle to left-hand needle, and P them, K2 rem sts from cable needle*, end with P2, K2, P2. Rep these 16 rows.

Cable patterns

Horseshoe cable   Twisted cable
Ribbed cable   Chain cable

Horseshoe cable Work over 8 sts. These samples are shown on a reverse st st background. Plain horseshoe cable (on right): *On 5th then on every 6th row* Place 2 sts on a cable needle in front of the work, K2, then K2 from cable needle; place 2 sts on cable needle behind work, K2, then K2 from cable needle. Reversed horseshoe cable (on left): *On 5th then on every 6th row* Place 2 sts on cable needle at back of work, K2, K2 from cable needle; place 2 sts on cable needle at front of work, K2, K2 from cable needle.

Twisted cable Work over a number of sts divisible by 9 + 3. This sample is shown on a reverse st st background. *Rows 1 and 3* *P3, K6*, end with P3. *Row 2 and all even rows* Work the sts as set. *Row 5* *P3, place 3 sts on a cable needle at front of work, K3, K3 from cable needle*, end with P3. *Row 7* As row 1. *Row 9* *P3, place 3 sts on cable needle at back of work, K3, K3 from cable needle*, end with P3. *Row 10* As row 2. Rep these 10 rows.

Ribbed cable Work over 7 sts. This sample is shown on a reverse st st background. *Row 1 (WS)* *P1 tbl, K1*, 3 times, end with P1 tbl. *Row 2* Place 3 sts on cable needle at front of work, K1 tbl, P1, K1 tbl, P1, work sts from cable needle as follows: K1 tbl, P1, K1 tbl. *Rows 3, 5 7 and 9* Work as row 1. *Rows 4, 6, 8 and 10* *K1 tbl, P1*, 3 times, end with K1 tbl. Rep these 10 rows.

Chain cable Work over a number of sts divisible by 10 + 4. Two cable needles are needed. *Rows 1, 3 and 5* *P4, K2, P2, K2*, end with P4. *Row 2 and all even rows* Work the sts as set. *Row 7* *P4, place the first of the following 6 sts on a cable needle at front of work, place next 2 sts on other cable needle at back of work, K2, K st from cable needle at front of work, K1, K sts from cable needle at back of work*, end with P4. *Row 9* Rep from row 1.

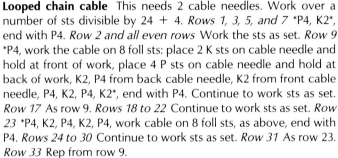

Looped chain cable This needs 2 cable needles. Work over a number of sts divisible by 24 + 4. *Rows 1, 3, 5, and 7* *P4, K2*, end with P4. *Row 2 and all even rows* Work the sts as set. *Row 9* *P4, work the cable on 8 foll sts: place 2 K sts on cable needle and hold at front of work, place 4 P sts on cable needle and hold at back of work, K2, P4 from back cable needle, K2 from front cable needle, P4, K2, P4, K2*, end with P4. Continue to work sts as set. *Row 17* As row 9. *Rows 18 to 22* Continue to work sts as set. *Row 23* *P4, K2, P4, K2, P4, work cable on 8 foll sts, as above, end with P4. *Rows 24 to 30* Continue to work sts as set. *Row 31* As row 23. *Row 33* Rep from row 9.

Irregular chain cable This needs 2 cable needles. Work over a number of sts divisible by 14 + 2. *Row 1* *P2, K5*, end with P2. *Rows 2, 3 and 4* Work sts as set. *Row 5* *P2, work the cable on next 5 sts: place next st on cable needle and hold at front of work, place next 3 sts on cable needle and hold at back of work, K1, K3 from cable needle, then K1 from 2nd cable needle, P2, K5*, end with P2. *Rows 6, 7 and 8* As row 2. *Row 9* *P2, K5, P2, work cable on next 5 sts*, end with P2. *Rows 10 to 16* As row 2. *Row 17* As row 9. *Rows 18, 19 and 20* As row 2. *Row 21* As row 5. *Rows 22 to 28* As row 2. *Row 29* Rep from row 5.

Chessmen cable Work over a number of sts divisible by 12 + 6. *Rows 1 and 3 (RS)* P6, *K6, P6*. *Rows 2 and 4* K6, *P6, K6*. *Row 5* P6, *place 3 sts on cable needle and hold at back of work, K3, K3 from cable needle, P6*. *Rows 6 and 8* K6, *P6, K6*. *Row 7* P6, *K6, P6*. *Rows 9 and 11* K6, *P6, K6*. *Rows 10 and 12* P6, *K6, P6*. *Row 13* *Place 3 sts on cable needle and hold at back of work, K3, K3 from cable needle, P6*, end with placing 3 sts on cable needle and hold at back of work, K3, K3 from cable needle. *Rows 14 and 16* P6, *K6, P6*. *Row 15* K6, *P6, K6*. Rep these 16 rows.

Butterfly wings Work over a number of sts divisible by 12 + 7. *Row 1 (WS)* K. *Rows 2, 4, 8 and 12* P1, *K1, P3, K1, P7*, end with K1, P3, K1, P1. *Rows 3, 5, 7, 9, 11 and 13* K1, *P1, K3, P1, K7*, end with P1, K3, P1, K1. *Rows 6 and 10* P1, *place 4 sts on cable needle and hold at back of work, K1, place the 3 P sts on left-hand needle and P them, K last st on cable needle, P7*, end with P1 instead of 7. *Row 14* P. *Row 15* K. *Rows 16, 18, 22 and 26* P7 *K1, P3, K1, P7*. *Rows 17, 19, 21, 23, 25 and 27* K7, *P1, K3, P1, K7*. *Rows 20 and 24* P7, rep from * to * as in row 6. *Row 28* P. Rep these 28 rows.

Making bobbles 1. This is one method of making bobbles and is usually worked on stocking stitch or reverse stocking stitch. *Row 1* Into the bobble st work (yfwd, K1) 3 times; there are now 6 sts on the needle, all made from the same st. Turn the work.

2. *Row 2 (WS)* Sl1 P, K rem 5 sts. Turn the work. *Row 3* Sl1, K rem 5 sts. Turn the work. *Row 4 (WS)* (P2tog) 3 times. 3 sts rem. Turn the work.

3. *Row 5 (RS)* Sl1, K2tog, psso. 1 st rem. Continue row normally.

4. These 5 rows, worked on 6 sts, make a bobble which stands out from the knitted background. For a larger bobble work on 8 sts, for a smaller bobble work on 4 sts, depending on the thickness of the yarn.

Simple trellis Work over 25 sts. *Row 1* P2, K6, P4, (K1, P1) 3 times, P4, K3. *Row 2* P2, C3B(P), C3F(P), (K1, P1) twice, C3B(P), C3F(K), P4, C3B(P). *Row 3 and all odd rows* Work the sts as set. *Row 4* P1, C3B(P), P2, C3F(P), K1, P1, C3B(P), K1, P1, C3F(K), P2, C3B(P), P1. *Row 6* C3B(P), P4, C3F(P), C3B(P), (K1, P1) twice, C3F(K), C3B(P), P2. *Row 8* K2, P6, C4B, (K1, P1) 3 times, C4B, P3. *Row 10* C3F(P), P4, C3B(P), C3F(K), (K1, P1) twice, C3B(P), C3F(P), P2. *Row 12* P1, C3F(P), P2, C3B(P), K1, P1, C3F(K), K1, P1, C3B(P), P2, C3F(P), P1. *Row 14* P2, C3F(P), C3B(P), (K1, P1) twice, C3F(K), C3B(P), P4, C3F(P). *Row 16* P3, C4F, (K1, P1) 3 times, C4F, P6, K2. Rep these 16 rows.

Mossy trellis Work over 28 sts. *Row 1 (RS)* P5, C4F, P10, C4F, P5. *Row 2 and all even rows* Work sts as set. *Row 3* P4, C3B(P), C3F(K), P8, C3B(P), C3F(K), P4. *Row 5* P3, *C3B(P), K1, P1, C3F(K)*, P6, rep from * to *, end with P3. *Row 7* P2, *C3B(P), (K1, P1) twice, C3F(K)*, P4, rep from * to *, end with P2. *Row 9* P1, *C3B(P), (K1, P1) 3 times, C3F(K)*, P2, rep from * to *, end with P1. *Row 11* *C3B(P), (K1, P1) 4 times, C3F(K)*, rep from * to *. *Row 13* K2 tbl, (K1, P1) 5 times, C4F, (K1, P1) 5 times, K2 tbl. *Row 15* *C3F(P), (K1, P1) 4 times, C3B(P)*, rep from * to *. *Row 17* P1, *C3F(P), (K1, P1) 3 times, C3B(P)*, P2, rep from * to *, end with P1. *Row 19* P2, *C3F(P), (K1, P1) twice, C3B(P)*, P4, rep from * to *, end with P2. *Row 21* P3, *C3F(P), K1, P1, C3B(P)*, P6, rep from * to *, end with P3. *Row 23* P4, C3F(P), C3B(P), P8, C3F(P), C3B(P), P4. *Row 24* As row 2. Rep these 24 rows.

Diamonds with bobbles *Row 1 (WS)* P1, K3, make bobble thus: K into front, back, front, back, front of next st – called wk bobble – then let it drop from needle, K2, P2, K1, P2, K2, wk bobble, K3, P1. *Row 2* K1, P3, K5tog tbl to complete bobble, P2, sl next 3 sts onto cable needle and hold at front of work, K2, sl P st from cable needle onto left-hand needle and purl it, K2 tbl from cable needle, P2, K5tog tbl, P3, K1. *Row 3* P1, K6, P2, K1, P2, K6, P1. *Row 4* K1, P5, C3B(P), P1, C3F(P), P5, K1. *Row 5* P1, K5, P2, K3, P2, K5, P1. *Row 6* K1, P4, C3B(P), P3, C3F(P), P4, K1. *Row 7* P1, K4, P2, K2, wk bobble, K2, P2, K4, P1. *Row 8* K1, P3, C3B(P), P2, K5tog tbl, P2, C3F(P), P3, K1. *Row 9* P1, K3, P2, K7, P2, K3, P1. *Row 10* K1, P2, C3B(P), P7, C3F(P), P2, K1. *Row 11* P1, K2, P2, K2, wk bobble, K3, wk bobble, K2, P2, K2, P1. *Row 12* K1, P1, C3B(P), P2, K5tog tbl, P3, K5tog tbl, P2, C3F(P), P1, K1. *Row 13* P1, K1, P2, K11, P2, K1, P1. *Row 14* K1, P1, K2, P11, K2, P1, K1. *Row 15* P1, K1, P2, K3, wk bobble, K3, wk bobble, K3, P2, K1, P1. *Row 16* K1, P1, C3F(P), P2, K5tog tbl, P3, K5tog tbl, P2, C3B(P), P1, K1. *Row 17* P1, K2, P2, K9, P2, K2, P1. *Row 18* K1, P2, C3F(P), P7, C3B(P), P2, K1. *Row 19* P1, K3, P2, K3, wk bobble, K3, P2, K3, P1. *Row 20* K1, P3, C3F(P), P2, K5tog tbl, P2, C3B(P), P3, K1. *Row 21* P1, K4, P2, K5, P2, K4, P1. *Row 22* K1, P4, C3F(P), P3, C3B(P), P4, K1. *Row 23* P1, K5, P2, K3, P2, K5, P1. *Row 24* K1, P5, C3F(P), P1, C3B(P), P5, K1. Rep these 24 rows.

Simple lozenge pattern Work over 14 sts. *Row 1* P5, K4, P5. *Row 2 and all even rows* Work sts as set. *Row 3* P4, C3B(P), C3F(P), P4. *Row 5* P3, C3B(P), P2, C3F(P), P3. *Row 7* P2, C3B(P), P4, C3F (P), P2. *Row 9* P1, C3B(P), P6, C3F(P), P1. *Row 11* P1, C3F(P), P6, C3B(P), P1. *Row 13* P2, C3F(P), P4, C3B(P), P2. *Row 15* P3, C3F(P), P2, C3B(P), P3. *Row 17* P4, C3F(P), C3B(P), P4. *Row 18* As row 2. Rep these 18 rows.

Trees Work over 33 sts. *Rows 1, 3, 5 and 7* P15, K3, P15. *Rows 2, 4, 6 and 8* K15, P3, K15. *Row 9* P14, C2R, K1, C2L, P14. *Row 10* K13, T2L, P3, T2R, K13. *Rows 11 to 14* Continue in this way, shifting the K sts making the branches by 1 st on every row. *Rows 15 and 16* Work the sts as set. *Row 17* Start the leaves on the K sts forming the branches. For each leaf work as follows, working rem sts as set: *Row 1* Make 1 at the edges of the K st (branch). *Row 2 and all even rows* P into made sts of previous row. *Row 3* K1, make 1, K1 (central st), make 1, K1. *Row 5* K2, make 1, K1 (central st), make 1, K2. *Row 7* K. *Row 9* Sl1, K1, psso, K3, K2tog, start 2 new branches as row 1. *Row 11* Sl1, K1, psso, K1, K2tog. *Row 13* Sl2, K1, P2sso. Continue 2 new branches, cross the sts as before and spread them to 4 sts from the central st. Work 2 rows without crossing, then work a leaf on each side. These leaves are shorter by 2 rows than the previous ones, so omit rows 5 and 9. As these are finished, start the top leaf: *Row 1* Make 1, K1 (central st), make 1. *Row 2 and all even rows* P into made sts of previous row. *Row 3* K1, make 1, K1 (central st), make 1, K1. *Row 5* Sl1, K1, psso, K1, K2tog. *Row 7* Sl2, K1, P2sso. End with 4 rows reverse st st.

Leaves Work over 18 sts. *Rows 1 and 3 (RS)* P18. *Rows 2 and 4* K18. *Row 5* P5, (T2R) twice, (T2L) twice, P5. *Row 6* K5, P1 tbl, K1, P1 tbl, K2, P1 tbl, K1, P1 tbl, K5. *Row 7* P4, T2R, P1, T2L, T2R, P1, T2L, P4. *Row 8* K4, P1 tbl, K3, P2 tbl, K3, P1 tbl, K4. *Row 9* P3, (T2R) 3 times, (T2L) 3 times, P3. *Row 10* K3, (P1 tbl, K1) twice, P1 tbl, K2, (P1 tbl, K1) twice, P1 tbl, K3. *Row 11* P2, (T2R) twice, P1, T2L, T2R, P1, (T2L) twice, P2. *Row 12 and all even rows* Work sts as set. *Row 13* P1, (T2R) 4 times, (T2L) 4 times, P1. *Row 15* As row 11. *Row 17* As row 9. *Row 19* As row 7. *Row 21* As row 5. *Row 23* P7, T2L, T2R, P7. *Row 24* K8, P2 tbl, K8. These 24 rows form the patt.

Decorated lozenge pattern Work on a panel of 22 sts. *Row 1 (WS)* K9, P4, K9. *Row 2* P9, C4B, P9. *Row 3 and all odd rows* Work sts as set. *Row 4* P8, C3B(P), C3F(P), P8. *Row 6* P7, C3B(P), P2, C3F(P), P7. *Row 8* P6, C2B, P4, C3F(P), P6. *Row 10* P5, C3B(P), P1, K4, P1, C3F(P), P5. *Row 12* P4, C3B(P), P1, C3B(P), C3F(P), P1, C3F(P), P4. *Row 14* P3, C3B(P), P1, C3B(P), P2, C3F(P), P1, C3F(P), P3. *Row 16* (P2, C3B(P), P2, C3F(P)) twice, P2. *Row 18* P1, (C3B(P), P4, C3F(P)) twice, P1. *Row 20* P1, K2, P6, C4B, P6, K2, P1. *Row 22* P1, (C3F(P), P4, C3B(P)) twice, P1. *Row 24* (P2, C3F(P), P2,C3B(P)) twice, P2. *Row 26* P3, C3F(P), P1, C3F(P), P2, C3B(P), P1, C3B(P), P3. *Row 28* P4, C3F(P), P1, C3F(P), C3B(P), P1, C3B(P), P4. *Row 30* P5, C3F(P), P6, C3B(P), P5. *Row 32* P6, C3F(P), P4, C3B(P), P6. *Row 34* P7, C3F(P), P2, C3B(P), P7. *Row 36* P8, C3F(P), C3B(P), P8. Rep these 36 rows.

Tree of Life – branches down Work on a panel of 15 sts. *Row 1 (RS)* P2, K1, P4, sl1 P ybk, P4, K1, P2. *Row 2* K2, sl1 P yfwd, K4, P1, K4, sl1 P yfwd, K2. *Row 3* P2, T2L, P3, sl1 P ybk, P3, T2R, P2. *Row 4* K3, sl1 P yfwd, K3, P1, K3, sl1 P yfwd, K3. *Row 5* P3, T2L, P2, sl1 P ybk, P2, T2R, P3. *Row 6* K4, sl1 P yfwd, K2, P1, K2, sl1 P yfwd, K4. *Row 7* P4, T2L, P1, sl1 P ybk, P1, T2R, P4. *Row 8* K5, sl1 P yfwd, K1, P1, K1, sl1 P yfwd, K5. *Row 9* P2, K1, P2, T2L, sl1 P ybk, T2R, P2, K1, P2. *Row 10* K2, sl1 P yfwd, K4, P1, K4, sl1 P yfwd, K2. Rep rows 2 to 10.

Tree of Life – branches up Work on a panel of 9 sts. *Row 1 (RS)* P3, K3, P3. *Row 2* K3, P3, K3. *Row 3* P2, T2R, K1, T2L, P2. *Row 4* K2, (P1, K1) twice, P1, K2. *Row 5* P1, T2R, P1, K1, P1, T2L, P1. *Row 6* K1, (P1, K2) twice, P1, K1. *Row 7* T2R, P1, K3, P1, T2L. *Row 8* P1, K2, P3, K2, P1. Rep these 8 rows.

Interlocked cables Work on a panel of 22 sts. *Rows 1 and 3 (WS)* K2, P2, K3, P2, K4, P2, K3, P2 K2. *Row 2* P2, K2, P3, K2, P4, K2, P3, K2, P2. *Row 4* P2, (C3F(P), P2) twice, (C3B(P), P2) twice. *Row 5 and all odd rows* Work sts as set. *Row 6* P3, C3F(P), P2, C3F(P), C3B(P), P2, C3B(P), P3. *Row 8* P4, C3F(P), P2, C4B, P2, C3B(P), P4. *Row 10* P5, (C3F(P), C3B(P)) twice, P5. *Row 12* P6, C4F, P2, C4F, P6. *Row 14* P5, (C3B(P), C3F(P)) twice, P5. *Row 16* P4, C3B(P), P2, C4B, P2, C3F(P), P4. *Row 18* P3, C3B(P), P2, C3B(P), C3F(P), P2, C3F(P), P3. *Row 20* P2, (C3B(P), P2) twice, (C3F(P), P2) twice. *Rows 22, 24 and 26* As row 2. Rep these 26 rows.

Jacquard knitting: 1st method: Twisting yarns 1. This is the method of changing colour for large motifs. Use a ball of yarn for each section and twist them when moving on to the next colour, so as not to leave a hole in the work. If the colour pattern changes vertically, take the new yarn behind the previous yarn.

2. If the colour pattern is diagonal with a slope to the right, pass the right-hand yarn in front of the left, when changing colour. On the wrong side of the work, the yarns twist automatically.

3. If the slope is to the left, twist the yarns on the wrong side of the work only. On the right side the yarns twist automatically.

2nd method: Stranding 1. When the design is small (over 3 stitches or fewer), carry the yarn not being used behind the work, crossing the yarns at the point of change so as not to leave a hole. Use both hands to carry the yarn, the first colour in the right hand, the second over the left thumb.

2. On the wrong side of the work, purl with the right hand while carrying the second yarn in the left hand. This can also be done with only one hand, dropping the yarns each time, but the resulting work is looser and less regular.

3. This is how the finished work appears on the wrong side. Make sure that an even tension is maintained, so that the work does not become pulled or puckered.

3rd method: Weaving 1. If there are more than 3 stitches in a group, the weaving method is used to avoid loose threads on the wrong side of the work.

2. On the right side of the work, hold the yarn not being used to the left. Put the right-hand needle into the stitch and pass the yarn not in use alternately under and over the working yarn.

3. Work in the same way on the wrong side of the work. Hold the thread not in use at the front of the work, weaving it under and over the working yarn. Take care to use only the working yarn to form the stitches on the needle.

Vertical rows The stranding or weaving method is used to work 2 to 5 sts in each colour. If the number of sts in each stripe becomes greater use a separate ball for each colour. This makes working with more colours easier too.

Horizontal rows Work 2 rows in each colour, keeping the number of rows even. A yarn not in use is carried up the side of the work and caught in the selvedge st every couple of rows.

Fancy rows Work over an even number of sts. It is worked in st st in three colours, A, B, and C, spacing them in the following way: 3 rows A, 2 rows C, 1 row B, 1 row C, 1 row B. Then work 1 row as follows: *1 st B, 1 st C, rep from * to end, then 1 row C. Rep these rows.

Rectangle stitch Work 3 sts in each colour, and change the colours every 4 rows (the number of sts and rows is optional). With a larger number of sts use a ball for each rectangle.

Two-colour Scotch stitch Work over a number of sts divisible by 10. Work 2 rows in each colour. *Row 1* In A, *P4, K1, P4, sl1 K-wise ybk tbl*. *Row 2* Work the sts as set, sl P-wise ytf the st slipped on previous row. *Row 3* In B, *P4, sl1 K-wise ybk tbl, P4, K1*. *Row 4* As row 2. *Row 5* Rep from row 1.

Star tweed stitch Work over a number of sts divisible by 4 + 1. *Row 1* In B, P. *Row 2* In A, K1, *sl1 P ybk, insert needle under loop before next st and K into it, sl1 P ybk, K1, pass first sl st over 3 sts, K1*. *Row 3* In A, P. *Row 4* In B, K3, *sl1 P ybk, insert needle under loop before next st and K into it, sl1 P ybk, K1, pass first sl st over 3 sts, K1*, end with K2. *Row 5* In B, P. Rep from row 2.

Two-colour patterns

Diagonal tweed stitch   Labyrinth stitch
Chevron stitch   Spaced chevron stitch

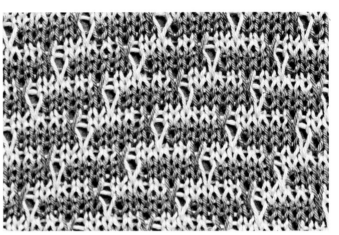

Diagonal tweed stitch Work over a number of sts divisible by 6 + 2 in 2 colours, A and B. Slip all sts P-wise with yarn on WS. *Row 1* In A, P. *Row 2* In B, K1, *sl2, K4*, end with K1. *Row 3* In B, K1, *P4, sl2*, end with K1. *Row 4* In A, K1, *K4, sl2*, end with K1. *Row 5* In A, K1, *sl2, P4*, end with K1. *Row 6* In B, K3, *sl2, K4*, end with sl2, K3. *Row 7* In B, K1, P2, *sl2, P4*, end with sl2, P2, K1. *Rows 8 and 9* In A, as rows 2 and 3. *Rows 10 and 11* In B, as rows 4 and 5. *Rows 12 and 13* In A, as rows 6 and 7. Rep from row 2.

Labyrinth stitch Work over a number of sts divisible by 6 + 1. Slip all sts P-wise with yarn on WS. Work 2 rows for each of the 2 colours, A and B. Cast on with A and work *Row 1* in P. *Row 2* In B, sl 1, *K5, sl1*. *Row 3 and all odd rows* Work the sts as set, sl the slipped sts. *Row 4* In A, K1, *sl1, K5*. *Row 6* In B, K4, *sl1, K5*, end with K2. *Row 8* In A, *K5, sl1 K-wise*, end with K1. *Row 10* In B, K2, *sl1 K-wise, K5*, end with K4. *Row 12* In A, K3, *sl1 K-wise, K5*, end with K3. *Row 14* Rep from row 2.

Chevron stitch Work over a number of sts divisible by 24 + 2 in 2 colours, A and B. Slip all sts P-wise with yarn on WS. *Row 1 (RS)* In B, K1, *sl1, K2*, end with K1. *Row 2* In B, K1, *P2, sl1*, end with K1. *Row 3* In A, K1, *K1, sl1, (K2, sl1) 3 times, K3 (sl1, K2) 3 times, sl1*, end with K1. *Row 4* In A, K1, *sl1, (P2, sl1) 3 times, P3, (sl1, P2) 3 times, sl1, P1*, end with K1. *Row 5* In B, K1, *K2, (sl1, K2) 3 times, sl1, K1, sl1, (K2, sl1) 3 times, K1*, end with K1. *Row 6* In B, K1, *P1, (sl1, P2) 3 times, sl1, P1, sl1, (P2, sl1) 3 times, P2*, end with K1. *Rows 7 and 8* In A, as rows 1 and 2. *Rows 9 and 10* In B, as rows 3 and 4. *Rows 11 and 12* In A, as rows 5 and 6. Rep these 12 rows.

Spaced chevron stitch Work over a number of sts divisible by 16 + 3 in 2 colours, A and B. Slip all sts P-wise with yarn on WS. *Row 1* In B, K1, sl1, *K3, sl1*, end with K1. *Row 2* In B, K1, sl1, *P3, sl1*, end with K1. *Row 3* In A, K4, *sl1, K3, sl1, K1, sl1, K3, sl1, K5*, end with K4. *Row 4* In A, K1, P3, *sl1, P3, sl1, P1, sl1, P3, sl1, P5*, end with P3, K1. *Row 5* In B, K3, *sl1, K3*. *Row 6* In B, K1, P2, *sl1, P3*, end with sl1, P2, K1. *Row 7* In A, K2, *sl1, K3, sl1, K5, sl1, K3, sl1, K1*, end with K1. *Row 8* In A, K1, P1, *sl1, P3, sl1, P5, sl1, P3, sl1, P1*, end with K1. Rep these 8 rows.

60

Soap bubbles Work over a number of sts divisible by 4 + 1 in 2 colours, A and B. *Row 1* In A, K. *Row 2* In A, P. *Rows 3 and 5* In B, K. *Rows 4 and 6* In B, P. *Row 7* In A, K2, *drop the next st and let it unravel 4 rows down, picking up A from the 2nd row, insert the needle into this st, under the 4 horizontal threads, in B, and K it keeping the threads behind it, K3*, end with K2. *Row 8* In A, P. *Rows 9 and 11* In B, K. *Rows 10 and 12* In B, P. *Row 13* In A, K4, *let the next st unravel and work it in A 5 rows down, as in row 7, K3*, end with K1. Rep from row 2.

Tile stitch Work over a number of sts divisible by 4 + 3 in 2 colours, A and B. *Rows 1 and 2* In A, K. *Row 3* In B, K1, *sl1 P ybk, K3*, end with sl1 P ybk, K1. *Row 4* In B, P1, *sl1 P yfwd, P3*, end with sl1, P1. *Rows 5 and 6* In A, K. *Row 7* In B, K3, *sl1 P ybk, K3*. *Row 8* In B, P3, *sl1 P yfwd, P3*. Rep these 8 rows.

Rows of beads Work over a number of sts divisible by 6 + 5 with 2 colours, A and B. *Row 1 (RS)* In A, K. *Row 2* In A, K1, *P3, K3*, end with P3, K1. *Row 3* In B, K1, *sl3 P ybk, K3*, end with sl3 P ybk, K1. *Row 4* In B, K1, P1, *sl1 P yfwd, P5*, end with sl1 P yfwd, P1, K1. *Row 5* In B, K. *Row 6* In B, K4, *P3, K3*, end with K1. *Row 7* In A, K4, *sl3 P ybk, K3*, end with K1. *Row 8* In A, K1, P4, *sl1 P yfwd, P5*, end with sl1 P yfwd, P4, K1. Rep these 8 rows.

Swallows' flight Work 2 rows for each of the colours, A and B. *Row 1 (WS)* In A, P. *Row 2* *K3, sl1 P ybk*. *Row 3* In B, sl1 P yfwd, *P3, sl1 P yfwd*. *Row 4* *K3, sl1 P ybk*. *Row 5* In A, P. *Row 6* K1, *sl1 P ybk, K3*, end with K2. *Row 7* In B, P2, *sl1 P yfwd, P3*, end with P1. *Row 8* K1, *sl1 P ybk, K3*, end with K2. Rep these 8 rows.

Two-colour patterns

Tweedy tapestry stitch	3/1 tweed stitch
Maltese Cross stitch	Knotted tweed stitch

Tweedy tapestry stitch Work over a number of sts divisible by 2 + 1 in 2 colours, A and B. Cast on required number of sts in A and P 1 row. *Row 1 (RS)* In B, K1, *ybk, sl1, K1*. *Row 2* In B, P. *Row 3* In A, K1, *yfwd, sl1, K1*. *Row 4* In A, P. *Row 5* In B, K2, *ybk, sl1, K1*, end with K1. *Row 6* In B, P. *Row 7* In A, K2, *yfwd, sl1, K1*, end with K1. *Row 8* In A, P. Rep these 8 rows.

3/1 tweed stitch Work over a number of sts divisible by 3 + 4 in 2 colours, A and B. Cast on required number of sts in B and K 1 row. *Row 1 (RS)* In A, K3, *ybk, sl1, K3*. *Row 2* In A, K3, *yfwd, sl1, K3*. *Row 3* In B, K1, *ybk, sl1, K3*, end with sl1, K1. *Row 4* In B, K1, *yfwd, sl1, K3*, end with sl1, K1. Rep these 4 rows.

Maltese Cross stitch Work over a number of stitches divisible by 4 + 3 in 2 colours, A and B. *Row 1* In A, P. *Row 2* In B, K3, *sl1 P ybk, K3*. *Row 3* In B, K3, *sl1 P yfwd, K3*. *Row 4* In A, K1, *sl1 P ybk, K3*, end with sl1 P ybk, K3. *Row 5* In A, K1, *sl1 P yfwd, K3*, end with sl1 P yfwd, K1. *Row 6* In B, as row 2. *Row 7* In B, P. *Row 8* In A, as row 4. Rep these 8 rows.

Knotted tweed stitch Work over an odd number of sts in 2 colours, A and B. *Row 1 (WS)* In A, K. *Row 2* In A, K1, *K1D, (work the st below the next st ie. the one worked in the previous row), K1*. *Row 3* In B, K. *Row 4* In B, K2, *K1D, K1*, end with K1. Rep these 4 rows.

62

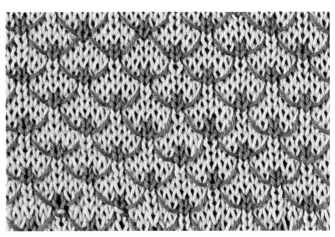

Lacy tweed stitch   Work over an odd number of sts in 2 colours, A and B. *Row 1 (WS)* In A, K. *Row 2* In B, K1, *sl1 P ybk, K1*. *Row 3* In B, K1, *sl1 P yfwd, K1*. *Rows 4 and 5* In A, K. *Row 6* In B, K2, *sl1 P ybk, K1*, end with K1. *Row 7* In B, K2, *sl1 P yfwd, K1*, end with K1. *Row 8* In A, K. Rep these 8 rows.

Royal quilt stitch   Work over a number of sts divisible by 6 + 3 in 2 colours, A and B. *Row 1 (WS)* In A, K1, P1, *sl5 P ybk, P1*, end with K1. *Row 2* In B, K. *Row 3* In B, K1, P to last st, K1. *Row 4* In A, K1, sl3 P ybk, *insert needle under the loose strand from row 1, K the next st bringing it under the strand to catch it, sl5 P ybk*, rep from * to last 5 sts, end with K the next st under the strand, sl3 P ybk, K1. *Row 5* In A, K1, sl3 P ybk, *P1, sl5 P ybk*, end with P1, sl3 P ybk, K1. *Rows 6 and 7* In B, as rows 2 and 3. *Row 8* In A, K1, *K next st under loose strand from row 5, sl5 P ybk*, end with K st under loose strand, K1. Rep these 8 rows.

Lacy quilt stitch   Work over a number of sts divisible by 6 + 2 in 2 colours, A and B. *Row 1 (WS)* In A, K1, *P1, K4, P1*, end with K1. *Row 2* In B, K1, *sl1 P ybk, K4, sl1 P ybk*, end with K1. *Row 3* In B, K1, *sl1 P yfwd, K4, sl1 P yfwd*, end with K1. *Row 4* In A, K1, *drop sl st in A to front of work, K2, K dropped st, sl2 P ybk, drop sl st in A to front of work, sl same 2 sts back onto left-hand needle, K dropped st, K2*, end with K1. *Row 5* In A, K1, *K2, P2, K2*, end with K1. *Row 6* In B, K1, *K2, sl2 P ybk, K2*, end with K1. *Row 7* In B, K1, *K2, sl2 P yfwd, K2*, end with K1. *Row 8* In A, K1, *sl2 P ybk, drop sl st in A to front of work, sl same 2 sts back onto left-hand needle, K dropped st, K2, drop sl st in A to front of work, K2, K dropped st*, end with K1. Rep these 8 rows.

Crown quilt stitch   Work over a number of sts divisible by 8 + 4 in 2 colours, A and B. *Row 1 (RS)* K3A, *K2B, K6A*, end with K1B. *Row 2* K1B, keep ybk, *P6A, K2B, keep ybk*, end with P3A. *Row 3* Take B under left-hand needle ready to work, K1B, *K6A (take right-hand needle under B strand of previous row, K1B) twice*, end with K3A. *Row 4* P3A, *K2B, keep ybk, P6A*, end with K1B. *Row 5* Rep from row 1, taking right-hand needle under B strand when working "K2B".

Pompons and tassels
Making a pompon
Making a tassel

Making a pompon 1. From a piece of cardboard cut out two circles the size of the finished pompon. Cut out a smaller circle from the centre of each of the larger circles. Place the two discs together and begin winding yarn neatly around them with one or more strands as shown.

2. Continue until the small central hole is filled, taking the last strands of yarn through with a blunt needle. Then, with a pair of sharp scissors, cut the yarn all round the outer edge of the discs, pushing the lower blade down between the two discs.

3. Separate the two discs enough to pass a strong strand of yarn between them. Tie a secure knot around the middle of the pompon to hold it together.

4. Carefully remove the two cardboard discs without pulling out any of the tufts of yarn. Fluff up and trim the tufts to make a thick round pompon. A multi-coloured pompon can be made by varying the colour of the yarn wound around the discs.

Making a tassel 1. From a piece of cardboard, cut a strip of the required depth for the tassel. Wind yarn around it until the tassel is thick enough. Pass a separate strand of yarn through the top of the tassel and tie a knot.

2. Cut through the yarn at the bottom edge of the tassel and remove the cardboard strip. Wind a strand of yarn around the top part of the tassel and knot it. Trim the ends of the tassel with scissors.

Beads on knitting 1. Before starting to work it will be necessary to thread the beads onto the yarn. Thread a normal sewing needle with a doubled length of strong thread. Pass the end of the yarn through the loop of thread and fold the end back. Thread beads onto the needle and push onto the yarn. Always leave a couple of beads over the yarn end while carrying out the threading to hold the yarn secure.

2. Having threaded the beads, start to work. In these samples the beads are placed with the wrong side of the work facing. Purl to the position of the bead, take the yarn back and slide a bead up the yarn and hold close to the work.

3. To hold the beads firmly, work the next stitch knitwise through the back of the loop. Purl to the position of the next bead and repeat steps 2 and 3.

4. When the work is completed the beads are on the right side of the work. The beads in this sample are spaced two stitches and three rows apart.

INTRODUCTION TO CROCHET

Crochet is a versatile craft with exciting design possibilities. This section contains not only the basic information for beginners in crochet, but also explains the more unusual traditional techniques such as filet crochet, Irish lace, hairpin and Tunisian crochet. In addition, the interesting stitch collection provides a rich source of inspiration.

Materials

Hooks A steel hook is used with very fine cotton, linen or silk yarns and sometimes with 3-ply yarn. The length is 13cm (5in) and the sizes available range from 0.6mm to 1.75mm.

An aluminium hook is used for working wool or synthetic yarns, lightweight to heavy. The length is 15cm (6in) and it is available in sizes 2mm to 7mm. The larger the number, the larger the size.

A tricot needle or hook is used for Tunisian crochet which forms a fabric similar to a knitted fabric. Because stitches are worked onto the hook on one row and off again on the next row, this hook has a knob at one end to prevent the stitches from slipping off. Usually made of aluminium, or sometimes wood, the hook is 30cm (12in) long and is available in sizes 2mm to 5mm.

A two-pronged fork is used for hairpin crochet to form a light airy fabric. The size of the forks varies according to width.

A plastic hook is used with rug yarn or fabric strips to make rugs. It is hollow, 13cm (5in) long and available in size 10mm.

Yarns Practically any kind of yarn can be used for crochet, natural or man-made, thin or chunky, ranging from very fine cotton to wool, string, rug wool or even cotton fabric torn into strips. However, some yarns are more suitable than others for certain types of crochet. Filet crochet, which is usually used for edgings or curtains, is best worked in a fine cotton yarn. Bouclé and tweed yarns are generally used for garments which are worked in a simple stitch as complicated patterned stitches would not benefit from a textured or multi-coloured yarn. Plain yarns, on the other hand, are used to show up textured stitches to best advantage, as the extra work required for these stitches can then be appreciated. Cotton or any suitable washable fabric can be used for crochet by cutting it into bias strips and joining them together with sewing or, for added interest, with knots. This can then be used to make bathroom rugs.

Tension

Before starting to crochet, whether you are following a pattern or creating an original design, work out an accurate tension sample using the chosen yarn and stitch for the garment. To begin with, use the hook size recommended on the ball band. Then if necessary, adjust the hook size to obtain the correct tension. The tension can also vary considerably if the yarn is held too tightly or too loosely. An experienced crochet worker will know by the 'feel' of the yarn how to hold it when working. A beginner will only be able to judge how tightly to hold the yarn by practising.

The number of stitches and rows determines the size of the crochet. If you have more stitches per 10cm (4in) on your sample than required, try a larger hook. If fewer, you should try a smaller hook.

Measuring the width Lay the sample on a flat surface and place pins vertically 10cm (4in) apart. For even greater accuracy, leave the work to 'rest' for a short while. Then count the number of stitches between the pins.

Measuring the length Lay the sample on a flat surface and place the pins as above but horizontally.

Continue testing until an accurate tension is obtained.

Abbreviations

beg	beginning	**rT**	reverse Tunisian stitch
ch	chain	**sp**	space
cl	cluster	**ss**	slip stitch
cont	continue	**st**	stitch
dc	double crochet	**sT**	simple Tunisian stitch
dec	decrease	**tr**	treble
dtr	double treble	**tr tr**	triple treble
htr	half treble	**Tss**	Tunisian slip stitch
inc	increase	**Ttr**	Tunisian treble
lp	loop	**WS**	wrong side
no	number	**yrh**	yarn round hook
patt	pattern	**ytf**	yarn to front
prev	previous		
qutr	quadruple treble		
rep	repeat		
req	required		
RS	right side		

An * indicates a repeat. Follow the instructions after the * once, then repeat from the * to the end of the row or as specified. Work the instructions within brackets [ ] the number of times stated. Alternatively, work the instructions within brackets [ ] all into the same place in the pattern. Square brackets [ ] and round brackets ( ) are used together in a pattern where a double set of brackets is required.

Note When working the foundation row of a crochet pattern, the stitches are worked into the chain. On subsequent rows, the stitches are worked by inserting the hook under the two horizontal threads at the top of the stitch in the row below, unless otherwise stated.

Starting to crochet

How to hold the crochet hook Hold the crochet hook in the right hand, between the thumb and index finger, placing the thumb on the flat part of the crochet hook. The yarn passes over the index finger and middle finger of the left hand, under the ring finger and around the little finger, folded towards the palm of the hand.

Making the first chain **1.** Hold the end of the yarn between the thumb and index finger of the left hand, closed between the ring and little fingers and the palm of the hand. Insert hook under thread from right to left and twist hook through 360° to make a loop. Insert the crochet hook from front to back under the yarn.

2. Pull hook through the loop to make first chain (ch).

Making a length of chain This is the starting point for all work. Make the first ch, holding the crochet hook horizontally. Then catch the yarn held in the left hand, this step is called yarn round hook (yrh), pulling it through the loop (lp) on the hook and drawing out a new ch.

Making a length of double chain This is used to make a firmer start to work. Make 2 ch. *Insert the crochet hook into the first ch, yrh, and pull through a lp, yrh and pull through the 2 lps on the crochet hook, closing the st. Repeat the step from * inserting the hook into the side of the st just made.

Slip stitch (ss) Miss first ch. *Insert the hook into the top of next ch, yrh, draw a lp through st and lp on hook, rep from *.

Double crochet (dc) 1. Insert hook into st, yrh and draw it through, so that there are 2 lps on the hook.

2. Yrh, draw it through both lps on the hook. Repeat these 2 steps into each st.

Reverse double crochet Work this in the normal way, but making a purl st by catching the yarn over the top instead of the bottom.

Trebles

Half treble	Double treble	Spaced treble stitches
Treble	Triple or quadruple treble	Relief treble stitches
		Turning the work

Half treble (htr) Yrh, insert hook into top of st, yrh and draw through a lp, yrh and draw through the 3 lps on the hook.

Treble (tr) 1. Yrh, insert hook into top of st, yrh and draw through a lp, yrh and draw through the first 2 lps on the hook.

2. Yrh again and draw through the last 2 lps on the hook, finishing the st.

Double treble (dtr) 1. Wind yarn twice round hook then insert hook into top of st.

2. [Yrh and draw through the first 2 lps on hook] 3 times to complete st.

Triple or quadruple treble (tr tr or qutr) Using the same method as for double treble, wind yarn on hook 3 or 4 times, then insert hook into top of st, then work instructions in square brackets 4 or 5 times.

Spaced treble stitches Insert the hook into the space between 2 sts instead of into the top of the st. Work normally, taking care not to pull the yarn too tight.

Relief treble stitches Insert the hook horizontally between one st and the next, then bring the hook back to the front of work through foll sp of the row below, then work normally, taking care not to pull the yarn too tight. This way of working results in a textured finish.

Slip stitch	*1 ch st to turn*
Double crochet	*2 ch sts to turn*
Half treble crochet	*2 ch sts to turn*
Treble crochet	*3 ch sts to turn*
Double treble crochet	*4 ch sts to turn*
Triple treble crochet	*5 ch sts to turn*

Turning the work Extra ch are worked at the end of a row before turning to bring the hook to the correct height for the next st being worked.

Counting the stitches If working in double crochet, the sts are counted along the top of the work. If working in trebles, it is easy to count the long sts.

Casting off 1. When the work is the desired length, work the last st in the usual way at the end of the row.

2. Work a chain st, lengthening the lp with the hook, cut the yarn and pull it through the last st.

Crossed treble stitch 1. *[Yrh] twice, insert hook into st, yrh and pull through lp, yrh and draw through first lp on hook, yrh and draw through first 2 lps on hook (3 lps on hook), yrh, miss next st, insert hook into next st, yrh and pull through lp.

2. [Yrh, draw through 2 lps on hook] 4 times, 1ch, 1tr into space where the 2 trs cross, 1ch, miss next st, rep from *.

Vertical triple treble Make 3ch to turn, insert hook into first ch, yrh, draw through lp [insert hook into next ch, draw through lp] twice, insert hook into next st along row, yrh, draw through lp [yrh, draw lp through first 2 lps on hook] 4 times to complete first st. Continue in this way, working into three lps along side of st.

Triple chain This is used as a quick foundation row for a piece of work. Make 4ch, 1tr in 4th ch from hook, *1tr in base of previous tr, rep from *.

Rolled triple Work on a base of ch. [Yrh] 5 times, insert hook in 5th ch from hook, yrh, pull through a lp, yrh, pull through 7 lps on hook (one at a time), *[yrh] 5 times, insert hook in next ch, yrh, pull through 7 lps on hook, rep from *.

Woven trebles Work over a background of trebles separated by 1ch sps. Cut contrast yarns into lengths long enough to weave vertically through the fabric, allowing extra for weaving and fringing. Use a blunt-ended needle with two lengths of yarn.

Crochet in rounds

Working in rounds	Working a flat circle
Working a square	Working a circle on a ring
	Tubular work

Working in rounds 1. Make 4ch, ss into first ch to form a ring.

2. Continue working, increasing at regular intervals to keep the work flat. *Round 1* Work 2dc in each ch. *Round 2* Work 2dc in every alt dc. *Round 3* Work 2dc in every 3rd dc. *Round 4* Work 2dc in every 4th dc. Continue in this way for size required.

Working a square Work as in rounds to end of round 1. *Round 2* Work [1dc in each of next 2dc, 1ch] 4 times, ss in first dc. *Round 3* [Work 1dc in each of next 2dc, 1dc/1ch/1dc all in corner ch] 4 times. Continue in this way working 1dc in each dc and 1dc/1ch/1dc in each dc at corner.

Working a flat circle 1. This is an alternative method of working in rounds. Make a loop with the yarn, winding it round the finger a couple of times, and work into the centre of it.

2. Work required number of dc round circle, over both strands. Pull loose end firmly to draw circle together and close ring with a slip st. Continue work on this base, increasing regularly as explained for working in rounds.

Working a circle on a ring For decorative motifs it is necessary to work on a plastic ring, covering it completely in dc. When this is done, continue to work normally.

Tubular work 1. Make a length of ch (the number of ch required will vary, depending on the circumference of the tube). Ss into first ch to form a ring.

2. Start the rows with 1, 2 or 3ch according to the st to be used.

3. Each row is completed with a ss worked into the top of the starting ch. This is important to keep changes of colour or pattern even.

Increasing
Increasing at edges
Increasing in middle of row

Single increase at each end of a row To increase at the beginning of a row, turn the work with a ch as required, then work 2 sts into the first st. Use the same method at the end of a row, working 2 sts into the penultimate st, then work the last st normally.

Increasing 2 stitches at each end of a row Turn work with ch required. Work 2 sts into each of first 2 sts, work to last 3 sts, 2 sts into each of next 2 sts, 1 st into last st.

Increasing at regular intervals If the sts to be increased are 1 st every row on the same side, work 2 sts into first or last st of every row.

Adding stitches at the beginning of a row Make the same number of ch as sts to be increased, plus the number of ch required for turning. Turn the work and work new sts in the pattern.

Adding stitches at the end of a row To keep increased sts made at both ends of row level, make provision for these sts on previous row. Make same number of extra ch as sts required. Work ss over new ch and cont in pattern. On next row cont to end in pattern, working over ss.

Single increase in middle of row To increase in the middle of a row, work twice into the same st.

Double increase in the middle of a row To increase 2 sts in the middle of a row, work 3 times into the same st. If this repeat is to be regular and symmetrical, choose a st and work twice into the st on either side of it.

Decorative increasing in the middle of a row Increasing can also be made using ch. On the wrong side of the work, choose the place for increasing. Then work a ch between sts at the chosen place. On the foll row, work into the ch.

Increasing evenly in the middle of a row If the increases are to be made at regular intervals, mark the st to be used with a contrast thread. To work the increase on the right, work twice into the st before the marked st. To increase on the left work twice into the st after the marked st.

Decreasing
Decreasing at edges
Decreasing in middle of row

Decreasing a stitch at the edge of a row 1. To decrease a st at the left-hand edge of a row, work to last 2 sts, miss next st, work into last st, then make turning ch.

2. To decrease a st on the right of the work, work the first st, miss the second st, and continue normally.

Decreasing trebles At the beginning of the row [yrh, insert hook into next st, yrh, draw through a lp, yrh, draw through 2 lps on hook] twice, yrh, draw through 3 lps on hook (1tr dec). At the end of the row, work the third and second sts from the end in the same way.

Decreasing any number of stitches at the edge of the work 1. To decrease at the end of the row leave the number of sts to be decreased unworked, then make turning ch.

2. To decrease at the beginning of a row work ss over the number of sts to be decreased, then make turning ch.

Decreasing at the beginning of row to form a sloping edge At the beginning of the row work the sts to be decreased as follows: 1ss, 1dc, 1htr, 1tr, then continue with the selected st. More sts can be worked of varying heights to give a longer slope.

Simple decreasing in the middle of a row To decrease a st in the middle of a row work 2 sts without completing them, leaving 3 lps on the hook, yrh and draw through all the lps together.

Decreasing more than one stitch in the middle of a row At the required position, work 3 sts without completing them, leaving 4 lps on hook, yrh and draw through all the lps together.

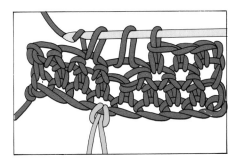

Repeat decreasing in the middle of work If the decreasing is to be repeated on following rows, mark the st to the side of that to be decreased with a contrasting thread, work this st together with the previous and following sts, finishing them all together.

Basic stitches

Double crochet	Albanian double crochet
Ribbed double crochet	Half treble
Treble	Double treble

Double crochet Make no of ch required plus 2 for turning. *Foundation row* 1dc in 3rd ch from hook, 1dc in each ch to end, turn. *Row 1* 2ch, miss first dc, 1dc in each dc to end. 1dc in 2nd of 2ch, turn. Rep this row for a fabric of double crochet.

Albanian double crochet Work the foundation row in dc. The 2nd and following rows are worked in dc by inserting the hook only into the front lp of each dc.

Ribbed double crochet Work the foundation row in dc. The 2nd and the following rows are worked only into the back thread of the dc. This is a softer version of Albanian double crochet, (taking the back instead of the front thread), but the result is different, being ridged and vertically elastic.

Half treble Make no of ch required plus 2 for turning. *Foundation row* 1htr in 3rd ch from hook, 1htr in each ch to end, turn. *Row 1* 2ch, miss first htr, 1htr in each htr to end, 1htr in 2nd of 2 ch turn. Rep this row for a fabric of half treble.

Treble Make no of ch required plus 3 for turning. *Foundation row* 1tr in 4th ch from hook, 1tr in each ch to end, turn. *Row 1* 3ch, miss first tr, 1tr in each tr to end, 1tr in top of 3ch, turn. Rep this row for a fabric of treble.

Double treble Make no of ch required plus 4 for turning. *Foundation row* 1dtr in 5th ch from hook, 1dtr in each ch to end, turn. *Row 1* 4ch, miss first dtr, 1dtr in each dtr to end, 1dtr in top of 4ch, turn. Rep this row for a fabric of double treble.

Fabric stitches

Alternate stitch   Crossed stitch
Ladder stitch   Leaf stitch
Exchange stitch   Crossed trebles

Alternate stitch   Work over a multiple of 2dc. *Row 1* 1ch, *miss 1dc, 1dc and 1tr into next st, rep from * to end, turn. *Patt row* 1ch, work 1dc and 1tr into each tr, turn. Rep this row to form patt.

Crossed stitch   Work over an odd no of dc. *Patt row* 1dc in first dc, *insert hook into same place as st just worked, yrh and draw loop through, insert hook into next st, yrh, and draw loop through, yrh and close st. Rep from * to end, turn. Rep this row to form patt.

Ladder stitch   Work over a multiple of 6dc. *Patt row* *1dc in each of next 3dc, 1dc in back lp of next 3dc, rep from * to end, turn. Rep this row to form patt.

Leaf stitch   Work over a multiple of 2dc. *Patt row* 1ch *miss 1dc, 2dc in next dc, rep from * to end, turn. Rep this row to form patt.

Exchange stitch   Work over an odd no of dc. *Patt row* 1dc in first dc, *miss 1dc, 1dc in next dc, pass hook in front of st just worked and work 1dc into missed dc, rep from * to end, turn. Rep this row to form patt.

Crossed trebles   Work over an odd number of tr. *Patt row* 3ch, *miss next tr, 1tr in next tr, 1tr in missed tr, rep from * to last 2 sts, 1tr in top of turning ch, 1tr in missed tr, turn. Rep this row to form patt.

Fabric stitches

Granite stitch   Perforated granite stitch
Diamond stitch   Lacy bricks

Granite stitch Work over odd no of dc. *Patt row 1* 1dc in first dc, *1ch, miss 1dc, 1dc in next dc, rep from * to end, turn. *Patt row 2* 1dc in first dc, *1dc in 1ch sp, 1ch, rep from * to last 2 sts, 1dc in 1ch sp, 1dc in last dc, turn. Rep these 2 rows to form patt.

Perforated granite stitch Work over an odd no of dc. *Patt row 1* 2ch, miss first dc, *1ch, miss next dc, work 1 double dc [insert hook into st, yrh, draw through 1 lp, yrh, draw through 1 lp, yrh and close st] into next dc, rep from * to end, turn. *Patt row 2* 2ch, 1 double dc in next 1ch sp, *1ch 1 double dc in next 1ch sp, rep from * to last st, 1 double dc in 2nd of 2ch, turn. *Patt row 3* 3ch, *1 double dc in 1ch sp, 1ch, rep from *, ending 1dc in second of 2ch, turn. Rep rows 2 and 3 to form patt.

Diamond stitch Work over an even no of dc. *Patt row 1* *Yrh, insert hook into first dc and draw 1 lp through, yrh, insert hook into next dc and draw 1 lp through, yrh and draw through the first 4 lps, yrh and close last 2 lps, 1ch, rep from * inserting hook into the same place as last part of st just worked, to end of row. 1tr into last dc, turn. *Patt row 2* 1dc into each 1ch sp, 1dc in top of 3ch, turn. Rep these 2 rows to form patt.

Lacy bricks Work over an odd no of chain. *Foundation row* 2htr in 3rd ch from hook, *miss next ch, 2htr in next ch, rep from * to end, turn. *Patt row* 2ch, *miss 2htr, 2htr in next sp between htr, rep from * ending miss 2htr, 2htr in top of 2ch, turn. Rep this row to form patt.

Raised rib stitch Work over a multiple of 3dc + 2dc. *Row 1* 1dc in each dc to end, do not turn. Break off yarn. Return to beg of row. *Row 2* 1dc in each first 2dc, yrh, insert hook from right to left around corresponding dc on foundation row, yrh then complete as a tr (raised tr), 1dc in each of next 2dc, rep from * to end, turn. *Row 3* 1dc in each st to end, do not turn. Break off yarn. Return to beg of row. *Row 4* 1dc in each of first 2dc, *1 raised tr around stem of previous raised tr, 1dc in each of next 2dc, rep from * to end, turn. Continue in this way working 2 rows on RS then 2 rows on WS, working all raised trs around stem of previous raised trs.

Louisa stitch Work over a multiple of 4dc + 2dc. *Row 1* 3ch, 1tr in each st to end, turn. *Row 2 (RS of work)* 1dc in each of next 2tr, *1 raised tr around each of next 2tr, 1dc in each of next 2tr, rep from * to end, turn. Rep these 2 rows to form patt.

Daniella stitch Work over a multiple of 2dc. *Row 1 and all odd rows (WS of work)* Work in tr. *Row 2* *1dc in next tr, 1 raised tr in next tr, rep from * to end. *Row 4* *1 raised tr in next tr, 1dc in next tr, rep from * to end. Rep these 4 rows to form patt.

Wide raised rib Work over a multiple of 6dc + 5dc. *Row 1* 1dc in each of next 5dc, *1 raised tr around next dc, 1dc in each of next 5dc, rep from * to end. *Row 2* 1dc in each of next 5dc, *1 raised tr around next raised tr, 1dc in each of next 5dc, rep from * to end. Rep row 2 to form patt, noting that on alt rows the raised trs are worked from front and then back of raised trs.

77

Fan stitches

Little fans Work over a multiple of 3dc + 1dc. *Row 1* Work 3ch (to count as first tr) *1ch, miss 2dc, 3tr in next dc, rep from* to last 3dc, 1ch, miss 2dc, 1tr in last dc, turn. *Row 2* 3ch (to count as first tr), 1tr into centre st below 1ch sp, 1tr in 1ch sp, *1ch, 1tr in next 1ch sp, 1tr in centre st below 1ch sp, 1tr in same 1ch sp, rep from * working last tr in top of 3ch, turn. *Row 3* 4ch, * 1tr in next 1ch sp, 1tr in centre tr below 1ch sp, 1tr in same 1ch sp, 1ch, rep from * to end, 1tr in top of 3ch, turn. Rep rows 2 and 3 to form patt.

Columns of fans Work over a multiple of 4dc + 1dc. *Row 1* 3ch, miss 2dc, 4tr in next dc, *miss 3dc, 4tr in next dc, rep from * to last 2dc, 1tr in last dc. *Row 2* 3ch, work 4tr in centre of each 4tr group, 1tr in top of 3ch. Rep row 2 to form patt.

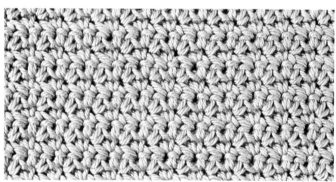

Little leaves stitch Work over a multiple of 2dc. *Row 1* *Miss 1dc, 1dc and 1tr into next dc, rep from * to end, turn. *Row 2* 1dc and 1tr into each dc to end of row, turn. Rep row 2 to form patt.

Little roses stitch Work over a multiple of 2dc. *Row 1* *Miss 1dc, work 2dc into next dc, rep from * to end, turn. *Row 2* *Miss 1dc, 2dc into next dc, rep from * to end, turn. Rep row 2 to form patt.

Stepped fans Work over a multiple of 4dc. *Foundation row* *Ss in next dc, 3ch, 1tr in next dc, 1htr in next dc, 1dc in next dc, rep from * to end, turn. *Row 1* Ss into each of first 3sts, *[1dc, 3ch, 4tr] all in next 3ch sp, rep from * to end, turn. Rep row 1 to form patt.

Wickerwork stitch Work over a multiple of 4dc + 1dc. *Row 1* [1dc, 2ch, 2tr] all into the first dc, *miss 3dc, [1dc, 2ch, 2tr] all in next dc, rep from * to end, turn. *Row 2* 2ch, *[1dc, 2ch, 2tr] all into next 2ch sp, rep from * to end, turn. Rep row 2 to form patt.

Little shell stitch Work over a multiple of 3dc + 1dc. *Row 1* 1dc and 2tr worked into first dc, *miss 2dc, 1dc and 2tr in next dc, rep from * to last 3dc, 1dc in last dc, turn. *Row 2* Work 1dc and 2tr into each dc to last dc, 1dc in last dc, turn. Rep row 2 to form patt.

Shell stitch Work over a multiple of 6dc + 1dc. *Row 1* 1dc in first st, *miss 2dc, 5tr into next dc, miss 2dc, 1dc in next dc, rep from * to end, turn. *Row 2* 3ch, 2tr into first dc, *1dc into 3rd tr of 5tr group, 5tr into next dc, rep from * ending with 3tr in last dc, turn. *Row 3* 1dc in first tr, *5tr in next dc, 1dc in centre tr of next 5tr group, rep from * working last dc in top of 3ch, turn. Rep rows 2 and 3 to form patt.

Large shell stitch Work over a multiple of 10dc + 1dc. *Row 1* 1dc in first st, *miss 4dc, 9tr into next st, miss 4dc, 1dc in next dc, rep from * to end, turn. *Row 2* 3ch, 4tr into first dc, *1dc into 5th tr of 9tr group, rep from * ending with 5tr into last dc, turn. *Row 3* 1dc in first tr, *9tr in next dc, 1dc in centre tr of next 9tr group, rep from * ending 1dc in top of 3ch, turn. Rep rows 2 and 3 to form patt.

Double shell stitch Work over a multiple of 6dc + 1dc. *Row 1* 1dc in first dc, *miss 2dc, in the next st work [3tr, 1dtr, 3tr], miss 2dc, 1dc in next dc, repeat from * to end, turn. *Row 2* 4ch, *leaving last lp of each tr on hook work 1tr in each of next 3tr, yrh, draw through all 4 lps on hook, 2ch, 1dc in next dtr, 2ch, leaving last lp of each tr on hook. Work 1tr in each of next 3tr, yrh and draw through all 4 lps on hook, 1dtr in next dc, rep from * to end, turn. *Row 3* 1dc in first dtr, *[3tr, 1dtr, 3tr] all in next dc, 1dc in next dtr, rep from * working last dc in 4th of 4ch, turn. Rep rows 2 and 3 to form patt.

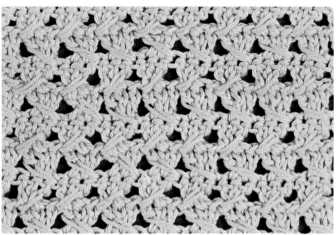

Jersey stitch   Work over an even no of dc. *Row 1 (WS of work)* 1dc in each dc to end, turn. *Row 2* 2ch, *miss 1dc, 1tr in next dc, passing in front of the st just worked work 1tr into missed dc, rep from * to last dc, 1htr in last dc, turn. Rep rows 1 and 2 to form patt.

Slanting alternate stitch   Work over a multiple of 3tr. *Row 1* 3ch, miss 1tr, *1tr in each of next 2tr, 1tr in missed tr, rep from * to last 2 sts, 1tr in each of last 2 sts. Rep this row to form patt.

Linked triples   Work over a multiple of 4tr + 2tr. *Row 1* 3ch, *miss 1tr, 1tr in each of next 3tr, 1tr into sp formed by missed tr, rep from * to last st, 1tr in top of 3ch, turn. Rep this row to form patt.

Double slanting stitch   Work over an even no of dc. *Rows 1 and 2* Work in dc. *Row 3* 1dc, *miss 1dc, 1dc in next dc, [yrh, insert hook in sp above missed dc, yrh, draw through lp] twice, yrh, draw through all 5 lps on hook, rep from * to last st, 1dc in last st, turn. *Row 4* 1dc in each st to end, turn. Rep rows 1 to 4 to form patt.

Eyelets Work over a multiple of 4tr + 2tr. *Row 1* 3ch, *miss next tr, 1tr in each of next 3tr, 1tr in sp formed by missed tr, rep from * to last st, 1tr in top of 3ch, turn. *Row 2* 3ch, 1tr in each st to end, turn. Rep these 2 rows to form patt.

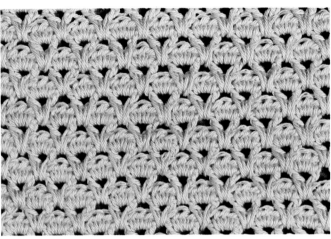

Alternate 'V' stitch Work over a multiple of 4dc. *Row 1* 3ch, miss next dc, *[1tr, 3ch, 1tr] all in next dc, miss 2dc, rep from * to last 3dc, [1tr, 3ch, 1tr] all in next dc, 1tr in last tr, turn. *Row 2* 1htr in first tr, *3htr in next 3ch lp, rep from * to end, 1htr in 3rd of 3ch, turn. *Row 3* 4ch, 1tr in first htr, *miss 3htr, [1tr, 3ch, 1tr] all into sp between 'V' st 2 rows below, rep from * end, [1tr, 1ch, 1tr] all in last htr, turn. *Row 4* 2ch, 1htr in 1ch lp, *3htr in next 3ch lp, rep from * ending 1htr in 1ch lp, 1htr in 3rd of 3ch, turn. *Row 5* 3ch, *[1tr, 3ch, 1tr] all into sp between 'V' st 2 rows below, rep from * ending 1tr in last dc, turn. Rep rows 2 to 5 to form patt.

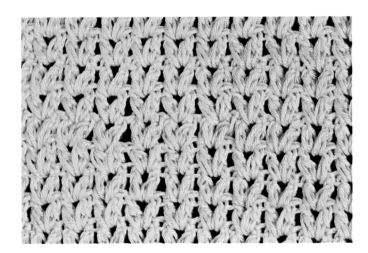

'V' stitch in columns Work over a multiple of 3tr + 1tr. *Row 1* 3ch, miss next tr, [1tr, 1ch, 1tr] all in next tr, *miss next 2tr, [1tr, 1ch, 1tr] all in next tr, rep from * to last 2tr, 1tr in last tr, turn. *Row 2* 3ch, work [1tr, 1ch, 1tr] all into each 1ch sp along row, 1tr in 3rd of 3ch, turn. Rep row 2 to form patt.

Twisted net stitch Work over a multiple of 2dc. *Row 1* 3ch, *miss next dc, [yrh] 5 times, insert hook in next dc, yrh, draw through lp, yrh, draw through all 7 lps on hook, 1ch*, rep from * to * to end, 1tr in last dc, turn. *Row 2* 3ch, work from * to * in row 1 into each 1ch sp, 1tr in 3rd of 3ch, turn. Rep row 2 to form patt.

Twisted stitch Work over a multiple of 4dc. *Row 1* 3ch, miss next dc, *1tr in next dc, along side of tr just worked work [yrh, insert hook into sp, yrh, draw through a lp] 5 times, yrh, draw through all lps on hook (a cluster), 2ch, miss 3dc, rep from * to last 2dc, 1tr in next dc, make a cluster around tr just made, 2ch, 1tr in last dc, turn. *Row 2* 3ch, *1tr in next 1ch sp, a cluster around tr, 2ch, rep from * ending 1tr in 3rd of 3ch, turn. Rep row 2 to form patt.

Lacy blocks Work over a multiple of 4tr + 2tr. *Patt row* 3ch, *miss next tr, 1tr in each of next 3tr, 1tr in missed tr, rep from * to last st, 1tr in top of 3ch, turn. Rep this row to form patt.

Little crosses Work over a multiple of 2dc. *Row 1* 1dc in first dc, *miss next dc, 1dc in next dc, 1dc in missed dc, rep from * to last dc, 1dc in last dc, turn. *Row 2* 1dc in each dc to end, turn. Rep these 2 rows to form patt.

Music sheet Work over any no of tr. *Patt row* 3ch, work 1tr in back lp only of each tr, 1tr in 3rd of 3ch, turn. Rep this row to form patt.

Thorn stitch Work over a multiple of 4dc plus 2dc. *Rows 1 and 2* 1dc into each st, turn. *Rows 3 and 4* 3ch, *miss next st, 1tr in each of next 3 sts, 1tr in missed st, rep from * to last st, 1tr in last st, turn. Rep these 4 rows to form patt.

Andalusian stitch Work over a multiple of 4dc plus 2dc. *Row 1* 3ch, *miss next dc, 1tr in each of next 3dc, 1tr in missed dc, rep from * to last dc, 1tr in last dc, turn. *Row 2* 1dc in each st to end, turn. Rep these 2 rows to form patt.

Lacy 'V' Work over a multiple of 2tr. *Row 1* 4ch, miss 1tr, 1tr in next tr, 1ch, *leaving last lp of each on hook, work 1tr in same place as last tr, miss 1tr, 1tr in next tr, yrh, draw through all lps on hook, 1ch to close, 1ch, rep from * to end, 1tr in top of 3ch, turn. *Row 2* 4ch, leaving last lp of each on hook, work 1tr in each of next 2 1ch sps, yrh, draw through all lps on hook, 1ch to close, 1ch, *leaving last lp of each on hook, work 1tr in same place as last tr, 1tr in next 1ch sp, yrh, draw through all lps on hook, 1ch to close, 1ch, rep from * to end 1tr in 3rd of 4ch, turn. Rep row 2 to form patt.

Linked oval stitch Work over a multiple of 3dc + 2dc. *Row 1* 3ch, miss next dc, 3tr in next dc, *miss 2dc, 3dc in next dc, rep from * to last 2dc, 1tr in last dc, turn. *Row 2* 4ch, leaving last lp of each on hook, work 1tr in each of next 3tr, yrh, draw through all lps on hook, 1ch to close, 1ch, rep from * to end, 1tr in 3rd of 3ch, turn. *Row 3* 1dc in first tr, 1dc in next 1ch sp, *1dc in next st, 2dc in 1ch sp, rep from * to end, turn. *Row 4* 1dc in each dc to end, turn. Rep rows 1 to 4 to form the patt.

Cluster squares Work over a multiple of 10dc + 3dc. *Row 1* 1dc in first dc, *leaving last lp of each on hook, work 4tr in next dc, yrh, draw through all lps, 1ch to close (a cluster made), 1dc in next dc, rep from * to end, turn. *Row 2* 1dc in each st to end, turn. *Row 3* 1dc in first dc, *1 cluster in next dc, 1dc in each of next 9dc, rep from * to last 2dc, 1 cluster in next dc, 1dc in last dc, turn. *Row 4* 1dc in each st to end, turn. *Rows 5 and 6* As rows 3 and 4. *Row 7* 1dc in first dc, *1 cluster in next dc, 1dc in each of next 4dc, rep from * to last 2dc, 1 cluster in next dc, 1dc in last dc, turn. *Row 8* 1dc in each dc to end, turn. *Rows 9 to 12* Rep rows 3 and 4 twice. These 12 rows form the patt.

Open dot stitch Work over a multiple of 6dc + 4dc. *Row 1* 1dc in first dc, *3ch, miss 2dc, 1dc in next dc, rep from * to end. *Row 2* 4ch, [yrh, insert hook in next 3ch lp, yrh, draw through lp] 5 times, yrh, draw through all lps on hook, 1ch to close cluster, *3ch, 1dc in next 3ch lp, 3ch, 1 cluster in next 3ch lp, rep from * to end, 1ch, 1tr in last dc, turn. *Row 3* 1dc in first tr, *3ch, 1dc in next 3ch lp, rep from * to end, working last dc in 3rd of 4ch, turn. *Row 4* 5ch, 1dc in next 3ch lp, *3ch, 1 cluster in next 3ch lp, 3ch, 1dc in next 3ch lp, rep from * to end, 2ch, 1tr in last dc, turn. *Row 5* 1dc in first tr, *3ch, 1dc in next 3ch lp, rep from * to end, 3ch, 1dc in 3rd of 5ch, turn. Rep rows 2 to 5 to form patt.

Cluster stitch Work over a multiple of 4dc + 1dc. *Row 1* 3ch, leaving last lp of each tr on hook, work 2tr in first dc, yrh, draw through 5lps on hook, 1ch to close cluster, *1ch, miss 1dc, 1dc in next dc, 1ch, miss next dc, leaving last lp of each tr on hook, work 5tr in next dc, yrh, draw through all lps on hook, 1ch to close cluster, rep from * to last 4dc, 1ch, miss 1dc, 1dc in next dc, 1ch, 3tr cluster in last dc, turn. *Row 2* 1dc in top of first cluster, *1ch, 5tr cluster in next dc, 1ch, 1dc in top of next cluster, rep from * to end, turn. *Row 3* 3ch, leaving last lp of each tr on hook, work 2tr in first dc, yrh, draw through all lps on hook, 1ch to close cluster, *1ch, 1dc in top of next cluster, 1ch, 1 5tr cluster in next dc, rep from * ending last rep 3tr cluster in last dc, turn. Rep rows 2 and 3 to form patt.

Dot stitch Work on a multiple of 2dc. *Row 1* 4ch, *miss next dc, [yrh, insert hook in next dc, draw through a long lp] 5 times, yrh, draw through all lps on hook, 1ch to close cluster, rep from * to last dc, 1tr in last dc. *Row 2* 4ch, *1 cluster in next sp between clusters, rep from * working last cluster after last cluster of previous row, 1tr in 3rd of 4ch, turn. Rep row 2 to form patt.

Pineapple stitch This stitch consists of working random clusters on a solid background, worked as follows: *Rows 1 and 2* Work in dc. *Row 3* Work in tr. The clusters are worked on *row 4* as follows: leaving last lp of each st on hook, work 5tr into corresponding dc in row 2, yrh, draw through all lps on hook, 1ch to close cluster. The other sts in this row are dc. These 4 rows form the basic st.

Open clusters This stitch consists of working random clusters on a solid background of dc. The clusters are worked into the corresponding st 2 rows below. To work a cluster, leaving last lp of each st on hook, work 5tr into dc, yrh, draw through all lps on hook, 1ch to close cluster.

Faggot stitch Work over a multiple of 2dc. *Row 1* 2ch, leaving last lp of each tr on hook work 1tr in each of first 3dc, yrh, draw through all lps on hook, 1ch to close, 1ch, *leaving last lp of each tr on hook work 1tr in same place as last tr, 1 tr in each of next 2dc, yrh, draw through all lps on hook, 1ch to close, 1ch, rep from * to last dc, 1htr in last dc. *Row 2* 1dc in each st to end. Rep these 2 rows to form patt.

Arches with dots Work over a multiple of 5ch + 1ch. *Row 1* 1dc in first ch, *5ch, miss 4ch, 1dc in next ch, rep from * to end, turn. *Row 2* *5ch, 1dc [yrh, insert hook into 5ch lp, yrh, draw through lp] 3 times, yrh, draw through all lps on hook (a cluster made), 1dc all in 5ch lp, rep from * ending 2ch, 1tr in last dc, turn. *Row 3* *5ch, [1dc, 1 cluster, 1dc] all in next 5ch lp, rep from * to end, 3ch, 1tr in 3rd of 5ch, turn. Rep rows 2 and 3 to form patt.

Lacy stitches

Net stitch Work over a multiple of 3ch + 8ch. *Foundation row* 1tr into 8th ch from hook, *2ch, miss 2ch, 1tr in next ch, rep from * to end, turn. *Row 1* 5ch, 1tr in next tr, *2ch, 1tr in next tr, rep from * to end, turn. Rep row 1 to form patt.

Lacy fan stitch Work over a multiple of 6tr + 9tr. *Row 1* 4ch, miss 1tr, 1tr in next tr, 1ch, miss 1tr, 5tr in next tr, *[1ch, miss 1tr, 1tr in next tr] twice, 1ch, miss 1tr, 5tr in next tr, rep from * to last 4tr, [1ch, miss 1tr, 1tr in next tr] twice, turn. *Row 2* 3ch, 1tr in next 1ch sp, 1ch, 1tr in next 1ch sp, miss 2tr, [1tr, 1ch, 1tr] all in next tr, *[1tr in next 1ch sp, 1ch] twice, 1tr in next 1ch sp, miss 2tr, [1tr, 1ch, 1tr] all in next tr, 1tr in next 1ch sp, 1ch, 1tr in next 1ch sp, 1tr in 3rd of 4ch, turn. *Row 3* 4ch, 1tr in next 1ch sp, 1ch, 5tr in next 1ch sp, *[1ch, 1tr in next 1ch sp] twice, 1ch, 5tr in next 1ch sp, rep from * ending 1ch, 1tr in next tr, 1ch, 1tr in 3rd of 3ch, turn. Rep rows 2 and 3 to form patt.

Square stitch Work over a multiple of 8tr + 7tr. *Row 1* 3ch, 1tr in each of next 6tr, *1ch, miss 1tr, 1tr in each of next 7tr, rep from * to end, turn. *Rows 2 and 3* 3ch, 1tr in each of next 6tr, *1ch, 1tr in each of next 7tr, rep from * to end, turn. *Row 4* 4ch, miss next tr, 1tr in next tr, [1ch, miss 1tr, 1tr in next tr] twice, *1ch, 1tr in next tr, [1ch, miss 1tr, 1tr in next tr] 3 times, rep from * to end, turn. *Row 5* 3ch, [1tr in next 1ch sp, 1tr in next tr] 3 times, *1ch, 1tr in next tr, [1tr in next 1ch sp, 1tr in next tr] 3 times, rep from * to end, turn. Rep rows 2 to 5 to form patt.

Lacy picots Work over a multiple of 5dc + 1dc. *Row 1* 1dc in first dc, *6ch, 1ss in 4th ch from hook (picot formed), 6ch, miss 4dc, 1dc in next dc*, rep from * to * to end. *Row 2* 9ch, *miss 4ch, 1dc in next ch, 6ch, 1ss in 4th ch from hook, 6ch, miss 1dc and 4ch, 1dc in next ch, rep from * ending 6ch, 1ss in 4th ch from hook, 2ch, 1dtr in last dc, turn. *Row 3* 1dc in first dtr, rep from * to * in row 1 working last dc in 5th of 9ch, turn. Rep rows 2 and 3 to form patt.

Cluster net Work over a multiple of 8tr + 7tr. *Row 1* 3ch, 1tr in each of next 6tr, *1ch, miss next tr, 1tr in each of next 7tr, rep from * to end, turn. *Row 2* 3ch, 1tr in next tr, 1ch, miss 1tr, leaving last lp of each on hook, work 5tr in next tr, yrh, draw through all lps on hook, 1ch to close cluster (a 5tr cluster made), 1ch, miss next tr, 1tr in each of next 2tr, *1ch, 1tr in each of next 2tr, 1ch, miss 1tr, 1 5tr cluster in next tr, 1ch, miss 1tr, 1tr in each of next 2tr, rep from * to end, turn. *Row 3* 3ch, 1tr in next tr, 1tr in next ch sp, 1tr in top of cluster, 1tr in next ch sp, 1tr in each of next 2tr, *1ch, 1tr in each of next 2tr, 1tr in next 1ch sp, 1tr in top of cluster, 1tr in next 1ch sp, 1tr in each of next 2tr, rep from * to end, turn. *Row 4* 4ch, miss next tr, 1tr in next tr, [1ch, miss 1tr, 1tr in next tr] twice, *1ch, 1tr in next tr, [1ch, miss 1tr, 1tr in next tr] 3 times, rep from * to end, turn. *Row 5* 3ch, [1tr in next 1ch sp, 1tr in next tr] 3 times, *1ch, 1tr in next tr, [1tr in next 1ch sp, 1tr in next tr] 3 times, rep from * to end, turn. Rep rows 2 to 5 to form patt.

Lacy dot stitch Work over a multiple of 6ch + 11ch. *Foundation row* 1tr in 8th ch from hook, 2ch, *miss 2ch, 1tr in next ch, rep from * to end, turn. *Row 1* 5ch, leaving last lp of each on hook, work 7tr in next tr, yrh, draw through all lps on hook, 1ch to close cluster, *2ch, 1tr in next tr, 2ch, 1 cluster in next tr, rep from * ending 2ch, 1tr in 3rd of 7ch, turn. *Row 2* 5ch, 1tr in top of next cluster, *2ch, 1tr in next tr, 2ch, 1tr in top of next cluster, rep from * ending 2ch, 1tr in 3rd of 5ch, turn. Rep rows 1 and 2 to form patt.

Fancy clusters Work over a multiple of 6tr + 1tr. *Row 1* 5ch, miss next 2tr, 4tr in next tr, remove hook from lp, insert hook into top of first tr, draw lp from 4tr through, 1ch to close cluster, *2ch, miss next 2tr, 1tr in next tr, 2ch, miss 2tr, 1 cluster in next tr, rep from * to last 3 sts, 2ch, 1tr in last st, turn. *Row 2* 3ch, *2tr in next 2ch sp, 1tr in top of next cluster, 2tr in next 2ch sp, 1tr in next tr, rep from * working last tr in 3rd of 5ch, turn. Rep rows 1 and 2 to form patt.

Mazzetti stitch Work over a multiple of 2dc + 1dc. *Row 1* 3ch [yrh, insert hook in next dc, draw through lp] 3 times all in same dc, yrh, draw through all sts on hook, 1ch, to close cluster, *1ch, miss next dc, 1 cluster in next dc, rep from * to last dc, 1tr in last dc, turn. *Row 2* 1dc in first tr, 1dc in next cluster, *1dc in next 1ch sp, 1dc in next cluster, rep from * ending 1dc in 3rd of 3ch, turn. Rep rows 1 and 2 to form patt.

Lacy stitches

Mesh stitch   Columns
Chequerboard stitch   Eyelet bands

Mesh stitch Work over a multiple of 4ch + 1ch. *Foundation row* 1dc in first ch, 3ch, miss 3ch, 1dc in next ch, rep from * to end, turn. *Row 1* 6ch, 1tr in next dc, *3ch, 1tr in next dc, rep from * to end, turn. *Row 2* 1dc in first tr, 3ch, 1dc in next tr, rep from * working last dc in 4th of 6ch, turn. Rep rows 1 and 2 to form patt.

Columns Work over a multiple of 3tr. *Row 1* 5ch, *miss next 2tr, 2dtr in next tr, 1ch, rep from * to end, 1dtr in top of 3ch, turn. *Row 2* 3ch, 1tr in first sp, *1tr in each of next 2dtr, 1tr in next 1ch sp, rep from * to end, 1tr in 4th of 5ch, turn. Rep these 2 rows to form patt.

Chequerboard stitch Work over a multiple of 6tr + 3tr. *Row 1* 3ch, 1tr in each of next 2tr, *3ch, miss 3tr, 1tr in each of next 3tr, rep from * working last tr in 3rd of 3ch, turn. *Row 2* 5ch, *3tr in next 3ch sp, 3ch, rep from * ending 2ch, 1tr in 3rd of 3ch, turn. *Row 3* 3ch, 2tr in 2ch sp, *3ch, 3tr in 3ch sp, rep from * ending 2tr in turning ch, 1tr in 3rd of 5ch, turn. Rep rows 2 and 3 to form patt.

Eyelet bands Work on a multiple of 2dc + 1dc. *Rows 1 and 2* Work 1dc in each dc, turn. *Row 3* 4ch, miss next dc, 1tr in next dc, *1ch, miss 1dc, 1tr in next dc, rep from * to end, turn. *Row 4* 1dc in first tr, *1dc in next 1ch sp, 1dc in next tr, rep from * ending 1dc in turning ch, 1dc in 3rd of 4ch, turn. Rep rows 1 to 4 to form patt.

Trapeze stitch Work over a multiple of 8tr + 7tr. *Row 1* 3ch, 1tr in each of next 6tr, *1ch, miss 1tr, 1tr in each of next 7tr, rep from * to end, working last tr in top of 3ch, turn. *Row 2* 3ch, 1tr in each of next 5tr, *1ch, miss 1tr, 1tr in next 1ch sp, 1tr in each of next 6tr, rep from * ending 1tr in top of 3ch, turn. *Row 3* 4ch, miss next tr, *1tr in each of next 6tr, 1tr in next 1ch sp, 1ch, miss 1tr, rep from * ending 1tr in each of next 4tr, 1tr in top of 3ch, turn. Continue in this way moving the 1ch sp 1 st on every row.

Mesh stitch with clusters Work over a multiple of 5ch + 1ch. *Foundation row* 1tr tr in 5th ch from hook, *4ch miss 4ch, [1tr tr, 2ch, 1tr tr] all in next ch, rep from * to last 6ch, 4ch, miss 4ch, 1tr tr in each of last 2ch, turn. *Row 1* 4ch, 1tr tr in next tr tr, *2ch, 1dc in next 4ch lp, 2ch, [1tr tr, 2ch, 1tr tr] all in next 2ch sp, rep from * ending 2ch, 1dc in last 4ch lp, 2ch, 1tr tr in next tr tr and top of 4ch, turn. *Row 2* 4ch, 1tr tr in next tr tr, *4ch, leaving last lp of each on hook, work 2tr tr in top of last tr tr, yrh, draw through all lps on hook (a 2tr tr cluster made), rep from * ending 4ch, 1tr tr in next tr tr and top of 4ch, turn. *Row 3* 4ch, 1tr tr in next tr tr, *4ch, 1tr tr in next tr tr, 2ch, 1tr tr in next tr tr, rep from * ending 4ch, 1tr tr in next tr tr and top of 4ch, turn. Rep rows 1 to 3 to form patt.

Arched mesh stitch Work over a multiple of 4dc + 1dc. *Row 1* 1dc in first dc, *5ch, miss 3dc, 1dc in next dc, rep from * to end, turn. *Row 2* *5ch, [1dc, 3ch, 1dc] all in next 5ch lp, rep from * to end, 2ch, 1tr in last dc, turn. *Row 3* 1dc in first tr, *5ch, 1dc in next 5ch lp, rep from * working last dc in 3rd of 5ch, turn. Rep rows 2 and 3 to form patt.

Crossed double treble stitch Work over a multiple of 6dc + 2dc. *Row 1* 1dc in each dc to end, turn. *Row 2* As row 1. *Row 3* 3ch, miss 3dc, 1tr tr in each of next 3dc, 1tr tr in each of 3 missed dc, rep from * to last dc, 1tr tr in last dc, turn. *Row 4* 1dc in first tr, 1dc in each tr tr to end, 1dc in top of 3ch, turn. Rep rows 1 to 4 to form patt.

Simple diadem stitch Work over a multiple of 8dc + 1dc. *Row 1* 6ch, *miss 3dc, [1tr, 1ch, 1tr] all in next dc, 3ch, miss 3dc, 1tr in next dc, 3ch, rep from * omitting 3ch at end of last rep, turn. *Row 2* 1dc in first tr, *3dc in next 3ch lp, 5dc in next 1ch lp, 3dc in next 3ch lp, 1ch, rep from * omitting 1ch at end of last rep and working 1dc in 3rd of 6ch, turn. *Row 3* 4ch, *miss 3dc, [into next dc work 2tr tr leaving last lp of each on hook, yrh, draw through all lps on hook, 1ch to close cluster, 1ch] 5 times, 1tr in next 1ch sp, 1ch, rep from * omitting 1ch at end of last rep and working 1tr into last dc, turn. *Row 4* 1dc in first tr, *1dc in each of next 3 1ch sp, 1ch, rep from * omitting 1ch at end of last rep and working 1dc into 3rd of 4ch, turn. *Row 5* 6ch, *[1tr, 1ch, tr] all in next 1ch sp, 3ch, 1tr in next 1ch sp, 3ch, rep from * omitting 3ch at end of last rep and working last tr in last dc, turn. Rep rows 2 to 5 to form patt.

Lace stitch Work over a multiple of 8dc + 1dc. *Row 1* 1dc in first dc, *3ch, miss 3dc, 1dc in next dc, rep from * to end, turn. *Row 2* 1dc in first dc, 1dc in next 3ch lp, 3ch, *1dc in same 3ch lp, 1dc in next dc, 1dc in next 3ch, lp, 3ch, rep from * ending 1dc in same 3ch lp, 1dc in last dc, turn. *Row 3* 1dc in first dc, *2ch, 1dc in next 3ch lp, 2ch, miss 1dc, 1dc in next dc, rep from * to end, turn. *Row 4* 1dc in first dc, 1ch, 1dc in first 2ch lp, 1dc in next dc, *1dc in next 2ch lp, 3ch, 1dc in next 2ch lp, 1dc in next dc, rep from * ending 1dc in next 2ch lp, 1ch, 1dc in last dc, turn. *Row 5* 1dc in first dc, *3ch, 1dc in next 3ch lp, rep from * ending last rep 1dc in last dc, turn. Rep rows 2 to 5 to form patt.

Beehive stitch Work over a multiple of 4dc + 1dc. *Row 1* 6ch, miss 3dc, 1tr in next dc, *3ch, miss 3dc, 1tr in next tr, rep from * to end, turn. *Row 2* 5ch, *1dc in next 3ch sp, 2ch, 1tr in next tr, 2ch, rep from * ending 1dc in next 3ch sp, 2ch, 1tr in 3rd of 6ch, turn. *Row 3* 6ch, 1tr in next tr, *3ch, 1tr in next tr, rep from * ending 3ch, 1tr in 3rd of 5ch, turn. Rep rows 2 and 3 to form patt.

Sunrise stitch Work over a multiple of 3dc + 1dc. *Row 1* 1dc in first dc, *4ch, miss 2dc, 1dc in next dc, rep from * to end, turn. *Row 2* 3ch [1tr, 2ch, 1tr] all in each 4ch lp to end, 1tr in last dc, turn. *Row 3* 1dc in first tr, 2ch, 1dc in next 2ch lp, * 4ch, 1dc in next 2ch lp, rep from * to end, 2ch, 1dc in top of 3ch, turn. *Row 4* 4ch, 1tr in first dc, [1tr, 2ch, 1tr] all in each 4ch lp, [1tr, 1ch, 1tr] in last dc, turn. *Row 5* 1dc in first tr, *4ch, 1dc in next 2ch lp, rep from * to end, 4ch, 1dc in 3rd of 4ch, turn. Rep rows 2 to 5 to form patt.

Half arch stitch Work over a multiple of 10dc + 5dc. *Row 1* 1dc in each of next 3dc, *3ch, miss 3dc, 1tr in next dc, 3ch, miss 3dc, 1dc in each of next 3dc, rep from * ending last rep 1dc in each of last 2dc, turn. *Row 2* 1dc in first 1dc, 1ch, miss next dc, 1dc in next dc, * 3dc in next 3ch lp, 1dc in next tr, 3dc in next 3ch lp, 1dc in next dc, 1ch, miss 1dc, 1dc in next dc, rep from * to end, turn. *Row 3* 3ch, 1tr in next 1ch sp, *3ch, miss 3dc, 1dc in each of next 3dc, 3ch, 1tr in next 1ch sp, rep from * to end, 1tr in last dc, turn. *Row 4* 3ch, 1tr in next tr, *3ch, 1dc in each of next 3dc, 3ch, 1tr in next tr, rep from * to end, 1tr in top of 3ch, turn. *Row 5* 1dc in each of first 2tr, *4dc in next 3ch lp, 1dc in next dc, 1ch, miss next dc, 1dc in next dc, 4dc in next 3ch lp, 1dc in next tr, rep from * to end, 1dc in top of 3ch, turn. *Row 6* 1dc in first dc, 1ch, miss next dc, 1dc in next dc, *3ch, 1tr in next 1ch sp, 3ch, miss 4dc, 1dc in next dc, 1ch, miss 1dc, 1dc in next dc, rep from * to end, turn. Rep rows 2 to 6 to form patt.

Row of 'V's Work over a multiple of 4dc + 2dc. *Row 1* 3ch, miss next dc, *[1tr, 2ch, 1tr] all in next dc, miss 3dc, rep from * ending 1tr in last dc, turn. *Row 2* 1dc in first tr, *1dc in next sp between tr, 3dc in next 2ch sp, rep from * to end, 1dc in top of 3ch, turn. *Rows 3 and 4* Work 1dc in each dc to end, turn. Rep rows 1 to 4 to form patt.

Single tulip stitch Work over a multiple of 4tr tr + 2tr tr. *Row 1* 4ch, *4tr tr in next tr tr, miss 3tr tr, rep from * to end, 1tr tr in top of 4ch, turn. Rep this row to form patt.

Double tulip stitch Work over a multiple of 5tr tr + 2tr tr. *Row 1* 4ch, miss 2tr tr, *leaving last lp of each on hook, work 3tr tr in next tr tr, yrh, draw through all lps to close cluster (a 3tr tr cluster formed), 2ch, 1 3tr tr cluster into same place as last cluster, miss 4 tr tr, rep from * ending last repeat miss 2tr tr, 1tr tr in top of 4ch, turn. *Row 2* 4ch, *[1 3tr tr cluster, 2ch, 1 3tr tr cluster] into next 2ch sp, rep from * to end, 1tr tr in top of 4ch, turn. Rep row 2 to form patt.

91

Jacquard work
Jacquard double crochet
Jacquard treble crochet

Simple vertical stripes, squares, zigzag patterns and many other designs can be worked using this method of crochet. It is a useful way of using up oddments of the same type of yarn to produce an interesting decorative effect. The method used is the same as in knitting, the difference being that in crocheted jacquard work the stitches are longer than in knitting and so less detailed designs are possible. For this reason, double crochet is most often used in this work.

The number of balls of yarn required depends on the number of colours being used. When changing colour, close the last stitch with the next colour, holding the yarn at the back of the work. When the colour changes are close together, the result is a firm, even fabric suitable for bags, mats etc. When using two colours, hold the working yarn over the left index finger and the second-colour yarn below this finger, working with the two yarns together so that each can be picked up in turn without tangling them. Always work with the right side of the work facing, or in the round, cutting the yarns at the end of each row.

Jacquard double crochet 1. Join in the second colour several stitches before it is needed, laying the yarn above the previous row and including it in the work.

2. Where the colour change is required, yrh with the second colour to close the last stitch. Lay the first-colour yarn along the previous row, including it in the work.

3. Whenever the colour being carried along the WS of the work is to be used again, pick it up during the closing stitch of the previous colour.

Jacquard treble crochet 1. Bring the second colour along the previous row, including it in the work as described for double crochet.

2. When changing the colour, yrh with the first colour, insert the hook and yrh with both colours, drawing both through, yrh with the new yarn, draw through both the single and the double stitch, yrh again and close the stitch.

A great variety of attractive motifs and all-over geometric patterns can be achieved with jacquard crochet. Remember that the colours not in use are carried along on the wrong side of the work. If a colour is to be carried more than three stitches, it is better to pick it up once every two stitches. If, however, all the stitches are worked over the yarn not in use, ie. the yarn is 'woven in', a reversible effect can be achieved, but it is not always possible to conceal the carried thread completely. For really neat jacquard work, it is best to work with small balls of yarn for each area of colour, especially where large and small areas of colour are combined.

When the colour changes are frequent, and more than two colours are being used, as in the Fancy rhombus pattern, it is advisable to use the weaving method of working.

In the following examples of jacquard motifs, one square corresponds to one stitch and one row. The motifs are worked in two colours, except for the Fancy rhombus, which is worked in three.

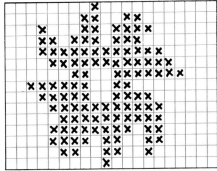

Bird This is worked over a base of 14 sts and a height of 15 rows.

Star This is worked over a base of 15 sts and a height of 15 rows.

Triangles This is worked over a base of 20 sts and a height of 12 rows.

Diamonds This is worked over a base of 20 sts and a height of 13 rows.

Fancy rhombus This is worked over a base of 20 sts and a height of 13 rows.

Multi-coloured patterns

Rows of double crochet   Random double crochet
Rows of treble crochet   Irregular rows

Rows of double crochet This is the simplest way of changing colour as it is done at the end of the row. The yarn is either cut or held aside to be picked up later. There is no RS or WS of the work, both sides being the same. When changing colour at the beginning of a row, make sure that the last stitch of the previous row is closed with the new colour.

Random double crochet This is useful for using up remnants of yarn. The colour change can be made in any position, perhaps several times in the same row. Take care to close the last stitch of one colour with the next colour to be used.

Rows of treble crochet As in double crochet the colour change takes place at the end of a row, the yarn being cut or kept aside to be picked up later. *Row 1* Work in tr. *Row 2 and following rows* Work in tr, inserting the hook between one stitch and the next. Again as for double crochet, there is no RS or WS to this work.

Irregular rows This stitch is shown using 3 colours, but it is possible to use more. The colour changes every row; cut the yarn at the end of the row, working the cut end into the first stitch of the next row, or keep it aside to be picked up a few rows later. *Row 1* Work in tr tr. *Row 2* Work in dc. *Row 3* Work in tr. Rep rows 1 to 3 to form patt.

Horizontal rib stitch Work on a base of ch stitch. *Row 1* In A, work in dc. Cut the yarn leaving at least 5cm/2in. *Row 2* In B, return to the beg and work in dc, inserting the hook into the back of the dc sts of previous row. Cut the yarn. *Row 3 and following rows* Rep row 2, changing colours each row. This stitch lends itself to cushion covers with fringes, as the threads at each end of the rows can be trimmed to the same length and knotted in twos to make a two-toned fringe.

Cock's foot stitch Work over a multiple of 2dc + 1dc using 2 colours. *Row 1* In A, 1dc in first dc, *1ch, miss next dc, 1dc in next dc, rep from * to end, turn. *Row 2* In A, 1dc in first dc, 1dc in next ch sp, *1ch, 1dc in next ch sp, rep from * ending 1dc in last dc, turn. Working 2 rows B and 2 rows A, rep these 2 rows to form patt.

Threaded chain stitch Work on a multiple of 2ch + 8ch in A. *Row 1* 1tr tr into 8th ch from hook, *1ch, miss 1ch, 1tr tr into next ch, rep from * to end, turn. *Row 2* 6ch, *1tr tr into next tr tr, 1ch, rep from * working last tr tr in 6th of 7ch, turn. Repeating row 2 forms an even mesh through which can be threaded a chain in colour B.

Multi-coloured mesh stitch Work over a multiple of 2tr + 1tr using 3 colours. *Row 1* In A, 4ch, miss 2tr, 1tr in next tr, *1ch, miss 1tr, 1tr in next tr, rep from * to end, turn. *Row 2* In B, 4ch, 1tr in next ch sp, *1ch, 1tr in next ch sp, rep from * to end, 1tr in 3rd of 4ch, turn. *Row 3* In C, 4ch, *1tr in next ch sp, 1ch, rep from * ending 1tr in 3rd of 3ch, turn. Rows 2 and 3 form the patt, working 1 row each of A, B, C.

Multi-coloured patterns
Three colour zigzag
Chequered stitch
Half loop stitch

Three colour zigzag Work over a multiple of 22ch + 1ch + 3 turning ch using 3 colours. *Row 1* In A, 1tr in 4th ch from hook, 2tr in same place as last tr, 1tr in each of next 8ch, leaving last tr of each on hook work [1tr in next ch, miss next ch] twice, 1tr in next ch, yrh, draw through all lps on hook, 1ch to close (a 5tr dec made), 1tr in each of next 8ch, 5tr in next ch, rep from * ending last rep 3tr in last ch, turn. *Patt row* In A, 3ch, 2tr in first tr, *1tr in each of next 8tr, 5tr dec, 1tr in each of next 8tr, 5tr in next tr, rep from * ending last rep 3tr in top of 3ch, turn. Working in stripes of 2 rows B, 2 rows C, 2 rows A, rep patt row to form patt.

Chequered stitch Work over a multiple of 6tr + 3tr using 2 colours. *Row 1* In B, 3ch, 1tr in each of next 2tr; in A, *1tr into each of the next 3tr; in B, work 1tr into each of the next 3tr, rep from * to end. *Row 2* As row 1, reading A for B and B for A. Rep these 2 rows, twisting the colours together at the end of each row, to form patt.

Half loop stitch Work over a multiple of 10tr + 8tr using 2 colours. *Row 1* In A, 4ch, miss next tr, *1tr in each of next 4tr, 1ch, miss 1tr, rep from * to end, 1tr in top of 3ch, turn. *Row 2* In A, 3ch, 1tr in first 1ch sp, *1ch, 4tr in next 1ch sp, rep from * to last 1ch sp, 1tr in last 1ch sp, 1tr in 3rd of 4ch, turn. *Row 3* In B, 4ch, *[2tr, 1ch, 2tr] in next 1ch sp, 1ch, rep from * to end, 1tr in 3rd of 3ch, turn. *Row 4* In A, 4ch, 1tr in next 1ch sp, 1ch, leaving last lp of each on hook, work 4tr around stem of tr just made, yrh, draw through all lps on hook, 1ch to close (a cluster made), 1ch, *4tr in next 1 ch sp, 1ch, 1tr in next 1ch sp, 1ch, a cluster around previous tr, 1ch, rep from * to end, 1tr in 3rd of 4ch, turn. *Row 5* In A, 3ch, 1tr in first 1ch sp, 1ch, *4tr in next 1ch sp, 1ch, rep from * to last 1ch sp, 1tr in last 1 ch sp, 1tr in 3rd of 4ch, turn. Rep rows 3 to 5 to form patt.

Multi-coloured patterns
Shell stitch
Two colour squares
Alternating square stitch

Shell stitch Work over a multiple of 8dc + 1dc using 2 colours. *Row 1* In A, 1dc in first dc, *miss 3dc, 7tr in next dc, miss 3dc, 1dc in next dc, rep from * to end, turn. *Row 2* In B, 3ch, 3tr in first tr, *1dc in centre tr of 7tr group, 7tr in next dc, rep from * ending 4tr in last dc, turn. *Row 3* In A, 1dc in first tr, *7tr in next dc, 1dc in centre tr of 7tr group, rep from * ending 1dc in top of 3ch, turn. Rep rows 2 and 3 to form patt.

Two colour squares Work over a multiple of 6tr + 3tr using 2 colours. *Row 1* In A, 3ch, 1tr in each of next 2tr, * 3ch, miss 3tr, 1tr in each of next 3tr, rep from * to end, turn. *Row 2* In A, ss in first tr, 2ch, *1tr in each of 3 missed tr on previous row working over the ch, 3ch, rep from * ending 2ch, ss in top of 3ch, turn. *Rows 3 and 4* In B, as rows 1 and 2. Rep rows 1 to 4 to form patt.

Alternating square stitch Work over a multiple of 6tr + 3tr using 2 colours. *Row 1* In A, 3ch, 1tr in each of next 2tr, *3ch, miss 3tr, 1tr in each of next 3tr, rep from * to end, do not turn. *Row 2* In B, ss into top of 3ch, 2ch, *1tr in each of 3 missed tr on previous row working over the ch, 3ch, rep from * ending 2ch, ss in last tr, turn. Working 1 more row B, 2 rows A, 2 rows B, rep rows 1 and 2 to form patt.

Rows and squares Work over a multiple of 6tr + 3tr. Using 3 colours, change colour every row. The pattern is made up of 3 rows of trebles (one for each colour) and 3 rows in Alternating square stitch (see page 97).

Rows of treble crochet Work over any no of tr using 3 colours. *Patt row and following rows* Work in trs, inserting the hook between one st and the next of the prev row. Change colours at the end of each row.

Three colour squares Work over a multiple of 6tr + 3tr using 3 colours. Work as given for Alternating square stitch (see page 97), changing colour every row.

Tile stitch Using 3 colours and changing colour every row, work as for Stepped fans stitch (see page 78).

Serpentine stitch Work over a multiple of 4tr tr + 1tr tr using 3 colours. *Row 1* In A, 4ch, miss next tr tr, 4tr tr in next tr tr, *miss 3tr tr, 4tr tr in next tr tr, rep from * to last 2tr tr, 1tr tr in last tr tr, turn. *Row 2* In A, 3ch, leaving last lp of each on hook, work 1tr tr in each of next 4tr tr, yrh, draw through all lps on hook, *3ch, leaving last lp of each on hook work 1tr tr in each of next 4tr tr, yrh, draw through all lps on hook, rep from * to last 3tr tr, 3ch, leaving last lp of each on hook work 1tr tr into each of last 2tr tr and 3rd of 3ch, yrh, draw through all lps on hook, turn. *Row 3* In B, 4ch, *4tr tr in next 3ch lp, rep from * to end, 1tr tr in last st, turn. Working 1 more row B, then 2 rows C, 2 rows A, 2 rows B, rep rows 2 and 3 to form patt.

Three colour dot stitch Work as given for Dot stitch (see page 84), using 3 colours.

Three colour fans Work over a multiple of 5dc + 2dc using 3 colours. *Row 1* In A, 3ch, 2tr in first dc, *miss 2dc, [3tr, 1ch, 3tr] all in next dc, rep from * to last 3dc, 3tr in last dc, turn. *Row 2* In B, 3ch, 2tr in first tr, *[3tr, 1ch, 3tr] all in next 1ch sp, rep from * to end, 3tr in 3rd of 3ch, turn. Working 1 row C, 1 row A, 1 row B, rep row 2 to form patt.

Three colour shell stitch Work over a multiple of 4dc + 1dc using 3 colours. *Row 1* In A, 1dc in first dc, *miss next dc, 3tr in next dc, miss next dc, 1dc in next dc, rep from * to end, turn. *Row 2* In B, 3ch, 1tr in first dc, miss 1tr, 1dc in next tr, *3tr in next dc, miss 1tr, 1dc in next tr, rep from * ending 2tr in last dc, turn. *Row 3* In C, 1dc in first tr, 3tr in next dc, miss 1tr, 1dc in next tr, rep from * working last dc in 3rd of 3ch, turn. Working 1 row each of A, B, C, rep rows 2 and 3 to form patt.

Afghan crochet
Square
Triangle

Square   1. In A, make 6ch, ss into first ch to form a ring. *Round 1* 3ch, into the circle work 2tr, (1ch, 3tr) 3 times, 1ch, ss into top of 3ch. Fasten off. *Round 2* Join B at any one of the 1ch spaces and work 3ch; into the same space work (2tr, 1ch and 3tr), *1ch, in the next ch space work (3tr, 1ch and 3tr)*; rep from * to * twice, 1ch, ss into top of 3ch. Fasten off.

2. *Round 3* Join C at any one of the spaces at a corner and work the 1st corner as in round 2; (1ch, 3tr into next space, 1ch, 1 corner into the next corner space) 3 times; 1ch, 3tr into next space, 1ch, ss in top of 3ch. Fasten off. *Round 4* Join D at any one of the corner spaces and work the 1st corner, [(1ch, 3tr into next space) twice, 1ch, 1 corner into next corner space] 3 times; (1ch, 3tr into next sp) twice, 1ch, ss into top of 3ch. Fasten off. *Round 5* Join E at any one of the corner spaces and work 1 corner [(1ch, 3tr into next space) 3 times, 1ch, 1 corner into next corner] 3 times, (1ch, 3tr in next sp) 3 times, 1ch, ss into top of 3ch. Fasten off.

Triangle (equal to ½ the square)   In A, make 5ch. *Row 1* Into 5ch work (3tr, 1ch, 3tr, 1ch and 1tr). Fasten off. *Row 2* Join B to the 3rd of 4ch, 4ch, 3tr into first ch sp, 1ch, into the next space work (3tr, 1ch and 3tr) (a corner), 1ch; into the last space work 3tr, 1ch and 1tr. Fasten off. *Row 3* Join C to the 3rd of 4ch, 4ch, 3tr into first ch sp, 1ch, 3tr into next ch sp, 1ch, 1 corner into next ch sp, 1ch, 3tr into next sp, 1ch, into the last sp work (3tr, 1ch, 1tr). Fasten off. *Row 4* Join D to the 3rd of 4ch, 4ch, 3tr into first ch sp (1ch, 3tr in next ch sp) twice, 1ch, 1 corner into next ch sp, (1ch, 3tr in next ch sp) twice, 1ch, into last sp work (3tr, 1ch, 1tr). Fasten off. *Row 5* Join E to the 3rd of 4ch, 4ch, 3tr into first ch sp, (1ch, 3tr in next ch sp) 3 times, 1ch, 1 corner into next ch sp, (1ch, 3tr in next ch sp) 3 times, 1ch, into last sp work (3tr, 1ch, 1tr). Fasten off.

Pentagon In A, make 4ch, ss into first ch to form a ring. *Round 1* 3ch, into circle work 1tr, (1ch, 2tr) 4 times, 1ch, end with ss into 3rd of 3ch. Fasten off. *Round 2* Join B with a ss in the space of 1ch, 3ch, into same space work (1tr, 2ch, 2tr) (1st corner), *1ch, into next space work (2tr, 1ch, 2tr)*; rep from * to * 3 times more (5 corners), 1ch, ss into 3rd of 3ch. Fasten off. *Round 3* Join C with a ss in a corner sp, work 1st corner in this same space, *(1ch, 2tr) into next space, 1ch, 1 corner at the next corner*; rep from * to * 3 times more; 1ch, 2tr in next ch sp. Fasten off. Continue in this way, keeping the corners one above the other, and working 2tr into the ch sps between corners separated by 1ch.

Hexagon Using A, make 6ch, ss into first ch to form a ring. *Round 1* 3ch, into circle work 1tr, (1ch, 2tr) 5 times, 1ch, ss into 3rd of 3ch, Fasten off. *Round 2* Join B with a ss, in a space of 1ch work 3ch, in the same space work (1tr, 2ch, 2tr) (1st corner), *1ch, into next sp work (2tr, 1ch, 2tr)*, rep from * to * 4 times more, 1ch, ss in 3rd of 3ch. Fasten off. *Round 3* Join C with a ss in a corner sp, work 1st corner in this same sp, *(1ch, 2tr) into next sp, 1ch, 1 corner in the next corner space*, rep from * to * 4 times more (6 corners); 1ch, 2tr in next ch sp, 1ch, ss into 3rd of 3ch. Fasten off. Continue in this way keeping the corners one above the other, working 2tr into the ch sps between corners, separated by 1ch.

Octagon Using A, make 6ch, ss into first ch to form a ring. *Round 1* 3ch, into the circle work 2tr, (1ch, 3tr) 3 times, 1ch, ss into 3rd of 3ch. Fasten off. *Round 2* Join B with a ss into 1ch sp, work 3ch, into same sp work 2tr, 1ch, 3tr (1st corner), *1ch, into next space work (2tr, 1ch, 2tr)*, rep from * to * twice more (4 corners), 1ch, ss into 3rd of 3ch. Fasten off. *Round 3* Join C with a ss into next ch sp, 3ch, into same sp work (1tr, 1ch, 2tr) (1st corner), *1ch, into next sp work (2tr, 1ch, 2tr)*, rep from * to * 6 times (8 corners), 1ch, ss in top of 3ch. Fasten off. *Round 4* Join D with a ss into 1ch sp, work a corner as in round 3, 1ch, 2tr into next sp, *1ch, (2tr, 1ch, 2tr) in next ch sp*, 1ch, 2tr in next ch sp, 1ch, rep from * to * 6 times more, ss in 3rd of 3ch. Fasten off. Continue in this way, keeping the corners one above the other, and working 2tr into the ch sp between corners, separated by 1ch.

Medallions
Star in a wheel
Hexagonal star
Six-pointed star

NOTE **On the following instructions work 3ch at beg of round in place of the first tr, when required.**

Star in a wheel Make 8ch, ss into first ch to form a ring. *Round 1* Into the circle work 6ch, (1tr, 3ch) 7 times, ss in 3rd of 6ch. *Round 2* Into first sp work (ss, 3ch, 1tr, 3ch, 2tr, 1ch); into each of next 7 3ch sp work (2tr, 3ch, 2tr, 1ch), ss in 3rd of 3ch. *Round 3* Ss in next tr and 3ch lp, *into next 3ch lp work (2tr, 3ch 2tr, 1ch), 1dc in next 1ch sp, 1ch, rep from * to end, ss in 3rd of 3ch. *Round 4* Ss in next 2 tr and 3ch lp, *into next 3ch lp work (3tr, 3ch, 3tr, 2ch), 1dc in next dc, 2ch, rep from * to end, ss in 3rd of 3ch. *Round 5* Ss in next 2tr and 3ch lp, *into next 3ch lp work (4tr, 3ch, 4tr, 3ch), 1tr in next dc, 3ch, rep from * to end, ss in 3rd of 3ch. *Round 6* Ss in next 3tr, *1dc in next ch sp, 1dc in each of next 4tr, 3ch, 1tr in next tr, 3ch, 1dc in each of next 4tr, rep from * working last 4dc in first 4ss. *Round 7* *1dc in next dc, 7ch, 1tr in next tr, miss 4dc, rep from * to end, ss in first dc. Fasten off.

Hexagonal star Make 8ch, ss into first ch to form a ring. *Round 1* Work (3tr, 2ch) 6 times in the circle, ss in top of 3ch. *Round 2* Work (1tr in each of next 3tr, 2ch, 1tr in 2ch sp, 2ch) 6 times, ss in top of 3ch. *Round 3* *3ch to count as first tr, 1tr in each of next 2tr (2ch, 1tr in next ch sp) twice, 2ch, rep from * to end, ss in top of 3ch. *Round 4* *3ch to count as first tr, 1tr in each of next 2tr, (2ch, 1tr in next ch sp) 3 times, 2ch, rep from * to end, ss in top of 3ch. *Round 5* *3ch to count as first tr, 1tr in each of next 2tr, 3tr into next space, (2ch, 1tr in next ch sp) twice, 2ch, 3tr into next sp, rep from * to end, ss in top of 3ch. *Round 6* *3ch to count as first tr, 1tr in each of next 8tr, 3tr in next ch sp, 2ch, 1tr in next sp, 2ch, 3tr in next ch sp, rep from * to end, ss in top of 3ch. *Round 7* *3ch to count as first tr, 1tr in each of next 11tr, 2tr into next sp, 3ch, 2tr into next sp, rep from * to end, ss in top of 3ch. Fasten off.

Six-pointed star Make 6ch, ss in first ch to form a ring. *Round 1* 3ch, 1tr, (3ch, 2tr) 5 times, 3ch into the ring, ss in top of 3ch. *Round 2* *1tr in next tr, 2tr in next tr, 4ch, rep from * to end, ss in top of 3ch. *Round 3* *2tr in next tr, 1tr in next tr, 2tr in next tr, 5ch, rep from * to end, ss in top of 3ch. *Round 4* *1tr in each of next 2tr, (1tr, 2ch, 1tr) worked in next tr, 1tr in each of next 2tr, 5ch, rep from * to end, ss in top of 3ch. *Round 5* *1tr in each of next 3tr, 3ch, 1tr in the 2ch sp, 3ch, 1tr in each of next 3tr, 4ch, rep from * to end, ss in top of 3ch. *Round 6* *1tr in each of next 3tr, 3ch, (3tr cluster, 3ch, 3tr cluster) in next tr, 3ch, 1tr in each of next 3tr, 3ch, rep from * to end, ss in top of 3ch. *Round 7* *1tr in each of next 3tr, 3ch, miss 3ch, (3tr cluster, 3ch) 3 times in next 3ch lp, 1tr in each of next 3tr, 3ch, rep from * to end, ss in top of 3ch. *Round 8* *1tr in each of next 3tr, 3ch, miss 3ch (3tr cluster, 3ch) twice in next 3ch lp, 3tr cluster in top of next cluster, (3tr cluster, 3ch) twice in next 3ch lp, 1tr in each of next 3tr, rep from * to end, ss in top of 3ch. *Round 9* *1tr in each of next 2tr, (3ch, 1dc in next 3ch lp) 3 times, 4ch, (1dc in next 3ch lp, 3ch) 3 times, rep from * to end, ss in top of 3ch. Fasten off.

NOTE **On the following instructions work 3ch at beg of round in place of the first tr, when required.**

Lacy star Make 6ch, ss in first ch to form a ring. *Round 1* 5ch, *(1tr, 2ch into ring) 7 times, ss in 3rd of 5ch; *Round 2* *4tr cluster in 2ch lp, 5ch, rep from * to end, ss in top of first cluster. *Round 3* *3ch, miss 2ch, (1tr, 5ch, 1tr) in next ch, 3ch 1dc in top of next cluster, rep from * to end. *Round 4* *3dc in next 3ch lp, 5dc in next 5ch lp, 3dc in next 3ch lp, rep from * to end, ss in first dc. Fasten off.

Festooned star Make 6ch, ss in first ch to form a ring. *Round 1* Work 14dc in ring. *Round 2* *1dc in next dc, 2dc in next dc, rep from * to end. *Round 3* *1dc in each of next 2dc, 2dc in next dc, rep from * to end. *Round 4* *1dc in each of next 6dc, 2dc in next dc, rep from * to end (32 sts). *Round 5* On the 32 sts work *5ch, miss 1dc, 1dc in next dc, rep from * to end (16 arches). *Round 6* Ss in each of next 2ch, 1dc in 5ch lp, *5ch, 1dc in next lp, rep from * ending with ss in first dc. *Round 7* Ss in each of next 2ch, 1dc in 5ch lp, *9ch, miss one 5ch lp, 1dc in centre of the next 5ch lp, rep from * ending with ss in first dc. *Round 8* Into each 9ch lp work (6dc, 2ch, ss in first ch, 6dc), ss in first dc. Fasten off.

Star with picots Make 6ch, ss in first ch to form a ring. *Round 1* Work 24dc into ring. *Round 2* 5ch, 1tr in first dc, 1ch, miss 2dc, *(1tr, 2ch, 1tr) in next dc, 1ch, rep from * to end, ss in 3rd of 5ch. *Round 3* *(3ch to count as first tr, 1tr, 2ch, 2tr) in next 2ch sp, 1dc in next ch sp, rep from * to end, ss in top of 3ch. *Round 4* *(3ch to count as first tr, 2tr, 1ch, 3tr) in next 2ch sp, 2dc in next dc, rep from * to end, ss in top of 3ch. *Round 5* *1dc in each st to 1ch sp, (1dc, 2ch, 1dc) in 1ch sp, rep from * to end, ss in first dc. Fasten off.

Beads on crochet

Double crochet with beads
Treble crochet with beads

Before starting work, thread the beads along the yarn, ready for use.
Double crochet: adding beads on WS row Insert hook and draw a lp through, slide a bead close to the 2 sts on the hook, yrh and close the st.

Double crochet: adding beads on RS row **1.** Slide a bead up to the st on the hook, insert hook into back of st.

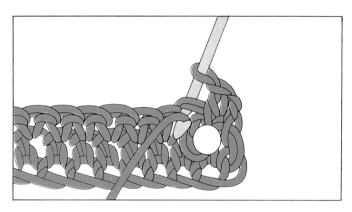

2. Yrh and draw a lp through to back of work, yrh and close the st. Slide another bead close to the st on the hook, and rep the process.

Treble crochet: adding beads on WS row Before closing the tr, slide a bead up to the 2 lps on hook, yrh and close the st.

Treble crochet: adding beads on RS row **1.** Yrh and slide a bead onto the hook, insert hook into st, yrh.

2. Draw through 2 lps on hook, passing the hook behind the bead. Yrh and close the st. Yrh, slide a bead onto the hook and rep the process.

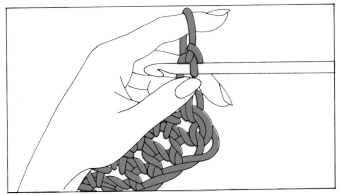

Crochet loops
Using a ruler
Using the index finger

Loop stitch using a ruler **1.** Use a ruler, or any suitable straight-edged flat object of the required height for the fringe. Work an initial row of dc, starting the loop stitch on the next row, *insert hook into first base st, yarn round the ruler (held in left hand) from front to back, yrh.

2. Draw the yarn through the st into which the hook was inserted, yrh again.

3. Close the st to make a dc*, rep from * to * in each st. Work the return row in dc. Rep these 2 rows. This method is used for extra long fringes.

Loop stitch using the index finger **1.** Work an initial row of dc. *Insert hook into st (or into back of st), and pass the yarn up and over the index finger of the left hand, yrh.

2. Draw the yarn through the st, yrh and close the st to make a dc*, rep from * to * into each st.

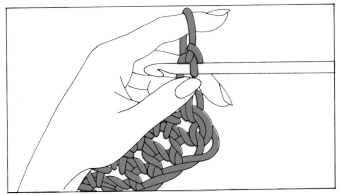

3. The st making the loop lies behind the work. Work the return row in dc. Rep these 2 rows.

Crochet edgings

Fan edging Work on a base of a multiple of 4dc + 1dc, using 3 colours. *Row 1* In A, 1dc in first dc, miss 1dc, *3tr into next dc, miss 1dc, 1dc in next dc, rep from * to end. Fasten off. *Row 2* In B, 3ch, 2tr into first dc, 1dc into centre of group of 3tr, 3tr in next dc, rep from * to end. Fasten off. *Row 3* In C, 1dc in centre of group of 3tr, *[2tr, 2ch, 2tr] into next dc, 1dc at centre of group of 3tr, rep from * to end. Fasten off.

Fan outline edging Work on a base of 4ch + 2ch, using 3 colours. *Row 1* In A, 1dc in each of first 2ch, *3ch, miss 2ch, 1dc in each of next 2ch, rep from * to end. *Row 2* In B, 1dc into each of first 2dc, *[1dc, 3tr and 1dc] into next 3ch lp, 1dc in each of next 2dc, rep from * to end. Fasten off. *Row 3* In C, 1dc in first dc, 2ch, 1dc in next dc, *2ch, miss 1tr, 1dc in next tr, 2ch, miss next dc, 1dc in next dc, 2ch, 1dc in next dc, rep from * to end. Fasten off.

Suspended fan edging Work on a base of a multiple of 4ch + 3ch, using 3 colours. *Row 1* In A, 1dc in first ch, *1ch, miss 1ch, 1dc in next ch, rep from * to end. Fasten off. *Row 2* In B, 4ch, 1tr into next dc, *1ch, 1tr in next dc, rep from * to end. Fasten off. *Row 3* In C, 1dc in first ch sp, 1tr in next dc, *5tr into next ch sp, 1dc in next ch sp, rep from * to end. Fasten off.

Open cluster edging Work on a base of 4ch + 3ch, using 4 colours. *Row 1* In A, 1dc in first ch, *1ch, miss 1ch, 1dc in next ch, rep from * to end. Fasten off. *Row 2* Attach B to first dc, 5ch, *1tr in each of next 2dc, 2ch, rep from * to last dc, 1tr in last dc. Fasten off. *Row 3* Attach C to 3rd of 5ch, 2ch, [1 3tr cluster, 3ch, 1 3tr cluster] in next 2ch lp, *2ch, 1dc into sp between 2tr, 2ch, work [1 cluster, 3ch, 1 cluster] into next 2ch lp, rep from * to end, 2ch, ss in top of last tr. Fasten off. *Row 4* Attach D to first 3ch sp, work [2dc, 2ch, 2dc] in first 3ch sp, *2dc in each of next 2ch sps, [2dc, 2ch, 2dc] in next 3ch sp, rep from * to end. Fasten off.

Three colour ribbon edging Work on a base of 4ch + 1ch, using 3 colours. *Row 1* In A, work 1dc in each ch to end. Fasten off. *Row 2* In B, 1dc in first dc, *7ch, miss 3dc, 1dc in next dc, 1ch, turn the work and into the arch work 4dc, turn the work, 1dc in each of next 4dc, 1dc into same place as dc worked into on row 1, rep from * to end, turn and fasten off. *Row 3* Attach C to last dc worked, *1dc in each of next 5dc, 1dc in side of next dc, 3dc in 3ch lp, rep from * to end, 1dc in last dc. Fasten off.

Crochet edgings

Festoon edging   Serpentine edging
Curved edging   Looped edging
Trefoil edging

Festoon edging Work on a base of a multiple of 5ch + 1ch. *Row 1* 1dc in first ch, *1ch, miss 1ch, 1dc in next dc, rep from * to end, turn. *Row 2* 1dc in first dc, *6ch, miss next dc, 1dc in next dc, rep from * to end, turn. *Row 3* 1dc in first dc, *into 6ch lp work [3dc, 3ch, ss into first ch, 3dc], 1dc in next dc, rep from * to end. Fasten off.

Curved edging Work on a base of a multiple of 10ch + 1ch. *Row 1* 1dc in first ch, *1ch, miss 1ch, 1dc in next dc, rep from * to end, turn. *Row 2* 2dc in first dc, *5ch, miss 4 sts, 1dc in next st, 7ch, 1dc into same st as last dc, 5ch, miss 4 sts, 2dc in next st, rep from * to end, turn. *Row 3* 1dc in each of first 2dc, 5dc into the 5ch lp, into the arches of the 7ch work [1ss, 1dc, 1htr, 2tr, 1htr, 1dc, 1ss], 5dc into the 5ch, 1dc in each of next 2dc, rep from * to end. Fasten off.

Serpentine edging Make 7ch. *Row 1* 1dc in 4th ch from hook, 1dc in each of next 3ch, turn. *Row 2* 7ch, 1dc in each of next 4dc, turn. *Row 3* 3ch, 1dc in each of next 4dc, turn. Rep rows 2 and 3 for length required ending with row 1. *Ending row* *1ch, 1dc in next 3ch lp, rep from * to end. Fasten off.

Looped edging Work on a base of a multiple of 8ch + 3ch. *Row 1* 1dc in first dc, *1ch, miss 1ch, rep from * to end, turn. *Row 2* 1dc in each of first 3 sts, *10ch, 1dc in each of next 5 sts, 2ch, turn, 1dc into 7th and 8th ch just worked, turn, 6ch, 1dc in each of next 3 sts, rep from * to end. Fasten off.

Trefoil edging Work over a multiple of 8ch + 1ch. *Row 1* 1dc in first ch, *1ch, miss 1ch, 1dc in next ch, rep from * to end, turn. *Row 2* 1dc in first dc, *3ch, miss 3 sts, into next 1dc work [5ch, ss into first ch – picot – 1tr tr, 1 picot, 1tr tr, 1 picot, 1dc], 3ch, miss 3 sts, 1dc into next dc, rep from * to end. Fasten off.

Filet crochet
Working a simple mesh
Working filled squares
Working open squares

Working a simple mesh Make required number of ch in a multiple of 3 + 5. For the foundation row work: 1tr into 8th ch from hook, *miss 2ch, 1tr into next ch, rep from * to end. On following rows work: 5ch (to count as first tr and 2ch sp), 1tr into next tr*, 2ch, 1tr into next tr, rep from * to end.

Working filled squares on foundation row To start the foundation row with a filled square, work 1tr into 4th ch from hook, then 1tr into each of next 2ch. For every subsequent filled square work 1tr into each of next 3ch. A filled square is made up of 2tr instead of a 2ch space with 1tr each side of it, making 4tr altogether.

Working open squares on foundation row Work 1tr into 8th ch from hook. For every subsequent open square work 2ch, miss 2ch, 1tr into next ch. An open square is made up of a 2ch sp with 1tr each side of it.

Working filled squares at beginning of rows At the beginning of the row make 3ch to count as first tr. Now work 2tr over either the next 2tr or 2ch sp, then work 1tr into next tr.

Working open squares at beginning of rows At the beginning of the row make 5ch to count as first tr and 2ch sp. Now miss either the next 2tr or 2ch sp, then work 1tr into next tr.

Working more than 1 filled square together After working a filled square at the beginning of a row, only 3tr are required for each subsequent filled square – 2tr over the central 2ch sp, then 1tr to complete the square.

Increasing an open square at the beginning of a row At the end of the previous row make 7ch, then turn. Work 1tr into first tr (last tr of previous row), then continue in pattern to end.

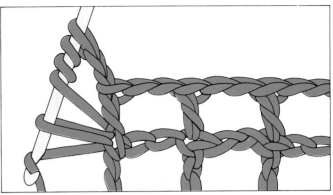

Increasing an open square at the end of a row Work in pattern to end of row, make 2ch, then work 1tr tr (yarn 3 times round hook) into base of last tr of row.

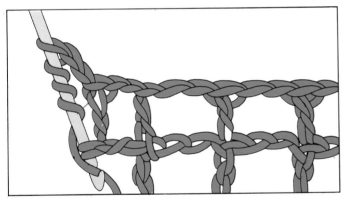

Increasing more than 1 square at the end of a row Increase first square at end of the row as already given above, then make subsequent squares as follows: 2ch, 1tr tr (yarn 3 times round hook) into corner formed by previous increased square.

Increasing a filled square at the beginning of a row At the end of the previous row make 5ch, then turn. Work 1tr into 4th ch from hook, 1tr into next ch, then 1tr into next tr (last tr of previous row), then continue in pattern to end.

Increasing a filled square at the end of a row Work in pattern to end of row, then work a tr tr into base of last tr of row, [work 1tr tr into base of previous tr tr] twice.

Graduated increasing At the beginning of the row work: 5ch (to count as 1tr and 2ch), then 1tr into first tr. At the end of the row work: 1tr as the last st of the row, then work 2ch and 1tr into same place as last tr.

Decreasing an open or filled square at the beginning of a row
Ss into the top of each of the first 4 sts of first square, make either 3ch for a filled square or 5ch for an open square, then work in pattern to end of row.

Decreasing an open or filled square at the end of a row Work in pattern to the last square of the row, then turn leaving the last 3 sts unworked. Make either 3ch for a filled square or 5ch for an open square, then work in pattern to end of row.

Graduated decrease of an open square at the beginning of a row Make 3ch instead of 5ch at beginning of row (omitting 2ch sp), then work 1tr into 2nd tr of row.

Graduated decrease of an open square at the end of a row Work to first tr of last square of row, work 1tr but do not work 2ch sp, then work 1tr into 3rd of turning ch.

Graduated decrease of a filled square at the beginning of a row Begin the row by working 1ss into first tr, 1dc into next st, 1htr into next st, then 1tr into next tr, work in pattern to end of row.

Graduated decrease of a filled square at the end of a row Work to first tr of last square of row, work 1tr into tr, 1htr into next st, 1dc into next st, 1ss into last st, turn and ss to first tr ready to begin next row.

Working corners 1. When working crochet borders in rounds the corners are worked by increasing stitches at regular intervals each side of the point. In filet crochet, which is generally worked backwards and forwards in rows across the width of the edging, a different method is used. If you have never worked a corner in filet crochet before, you will notice that the pattern changes at the corner enabling a symmetrical pattern to be worked without spoiling the allover design. In the example you will notice that the last 8 rows are shown in the chart, and that there is a heavier line, forming a step pattern, running diagonally to the corner. The heavier line shows where you must turn the work to form the corner, ie. on the first row work 1 filled square, 5 open squares, then 1 filled square, turn and leave any remaining squares unworked. On the next row work 3 filled squares, 3 open squares, then 1 filled square. Turn again and work 1 filled, 2 open and 2 filled squares – you have again reached the heavier line so turn and work back by working 2 open, 1 filled, 1 open and 1 filled square.

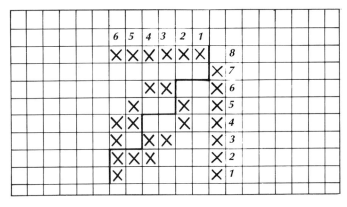

2. Continue in this way, working 2 fewer squares on every 2 rows until the last single square (1 open square) has been worked.

3. At the end of the last row, turn the work so that the right side is facing, then ss along to the left-hand side of the top square.

4. Turn work 90° so that stitch still on hook is at the right-hand edge. Working along side edges of previous corner rows, work the first row of the 2nd side by making 1 filled and 1 open square, ss to corner to secure end of row.

5. Ss along the top of the next stitch to bring the yarn to the appropriate point to start the next row.

6. Turn and work the 2nd row by working 1 open and 1 filled square. Then continue in this way, working extra squares every 2 rows until the corner is complete.

Irish crochet

Picot and arch stitch Make required number of ch, a multiple of 4 + 2. *Row 1* 1dc into 2nd ch from hook, *5ch, miss 3ch, 1dc into next ch, rep from * to end. *Row 2* 4ch, 1dc into first 5ch arch, *5ch, 1dc into next arch, rep from * to last arch, 2ch, 1tr into last dc. *Row 3* 3dc into 2ch sp, *into 5ch arch work [3dc, 4ch, 1ss into first of 4ch, 2dc, 4ch, 1ss into first of 4ch, 2dc], rep from * to end, 4ch, 3dc into 4ch sp. *Row 4* 1dc into first dc, *5ch, 1dc between central 2dc of arch, rep from * to end, working last dc into end dc. Rep rows 2 to 4 to form patt.

Picot grill stitch Make required number of ch, a multiple of 5 + 2. *Row 1* 1dc into 2nd ch from hook, *5ch, 1ss into 3rd ch from hook to form picot, 4ch, 1ss into 3rd ch from hook to form picot, 2ch, miss 4ch, 1dc into next ch, rep from * to end. *Row 2* 4ch, *into 1ch sp between picots work [1dc, 1tr, 1dc], 5ch, 1ss into 3rd ch from hook, 4ch, 1ss into 3rd ch from hook, 2ch, rep from * to last arch, into 1ch sp between picots work [1dc, 1tr, 1dc], 2ch, 1tr into last dc. *Row 3* 1dc into top of tr of previous row, *5ch, 1ss into 3rd ch from hook, 4ch, 1ss into 3rd ch from hook, 2ch, 1dc into 1ch sp between picots, rep from * to end, working last dc into 2nd of 4 turning ch. Rep rows 2 and 3 to form patt.

Scattered picot stitch Make required number of ch, a multiple of 4 + 1. *Row 1* 1tr tr into 4th ch from hook, 1 picot (3ch, 1ss into first of 3ch), into same ch as tr tr work [1tr tr, 1ch, 1tr tr], *miss next 3ch, into next ch work [1tr tr, 1 picot, 1tr tr, 1ch, 1tr tr], rep from * to end. *Row 2* 3ch, *into 1ch sp between tr tr work [1tr tr, 1 picot, 1tr tr, 1ch, 1tr tr], rep from * to end, 1tr tr into top of turning ch. Rep row 2 to form patt.

Diamond picot stitch Make required number of ch, a multiple of 5 + 2. *Row 1* 1dc into 2nd ch from hook, 7ch, 1ss into 5th ch from hook, 8ch, 1ss into 5th ch from hook, 2ch, miss 4ch, 1dc into next ch, rep from * to end. *Row 2* 7ch, 1ss into 5th ch from hook, [8ch, 1ss into 5th ch from hook] twice, 2ch, 1dc into central 3ch of first arch, *7ch, 1ss into 5th ch from hook, 8ch, 1ss into 5th ch from hook, 2ch, 1dc into central 3ch of next arch, rep from * to end. Rep row 2 to form patt.

Gothic stitch Make required number of ch, a multiple of 4 + 2. *Row 1* 1dc into 2nd ch from hook, *8ch, 1ss into 5th ch from hook, 3ch, miss 3ch, 1dc into next ch, rep from * to end. *Row 2* *8ch, 1ss into 5th ch from hook, 3ch, 1dc into 3rd ch of arch (st before next picot), rep from * to end. Rep row 2 to form patt.

Single mesh stitch Make required number of ch, a multiple of 4 + 10. *Row 1* 1tr into 10th ch from hook, *4ch, miss 3ch, 1tr into next ch, rep from * to end. *Row 2* 8ch, 1tr into first sp, *4ch, 1tr into next sp, rep from * to end. Rep row 2 to form patt.

Irish crochet edgings

Crown edging   Crested edging
Convoluted edging   Stepped picot edging
Fancy loop edging   Simple loop edging

Crown edging Make required number of ch, a multiple of 6 + 1. *Row 1* 1dc into 2nd ch from hook, 1dc into each ch to end. *Row 2* 1dc into first dc, *3ch, miss 2dc, [1tr, 5ch, 1tr] into next dc, 3ch, miss 2dc, 1dc into next dc, rep from * to end. *Row 3* Ss to 5ch arch, into each 5ch arch work 4tr, [4ch, 1ss into first of 4ch] 3 times, then 4tr. Fasten off.

Crested edging Make required number of ch, a multiple of 18 + 5. *Row 1* 1tr into 8th ch from hook, *2ch, miss 2ch, 1tr into next ch, rep from * to end. *Row 2* 1dc into first 2ch sp, *5ch, 1dc into next 2ch sp, 1htr into next tr, [1tr and 1dtr] into next 2ch sp, 1tr tr into next tr, [4ch, 1ss into first 4ch] 5 times, 1htr into top of tr tr, 1tr tr into same tr as previous tr tr, [1dtr and 1tr] into next 2ch sp, 1htr into next tr, 1dc into next 2ch sp, rep from * to last 2ch sp, 5ch, 1dc into last sp. Fasten off.

Convoluted edging Make required number of ch, a multiple of 5 + 2. *Row 1 (WS)* 1dc into 2nd ch from hook, 1dc into each ch to end. *Row 2* 1dc into first dc, *[4ch, 1ss into first of 4ch] 3 times, miss 1dc, 3tr tr into next dc, miss 2dc, 1dc into next dc, rep from * to end. Fasten off.

Stepped picot edging Make required number of ch, a multiple of 12 + 4. *Row 1 (WS)* 1tr into 6th ch from hook, *1ch, miss 1ch, 1tr into next ch, rep from * to end. *Row 2* 1dc into first tr, *[1dc into next 1ch sp, 1dc into next tr] twice, 1ch, 1tr into next tr, 1 picot (4ch, 1ss into first of 4ch), 1dtr into next tr, 1 picot, 1tr tr into next tr, 4 picots, 1dc into next tr, rep from * to end. Fasten off.

Fancy loop edging Make required number of ch, a multiple of 6 + 2. *Row 1 (RS)* 1tr into 8th ch from hook, *2ch, miss 2ch, 1tr into next ch, rep from * to end. Break off yarn. *Row 2* With right side still facing, rejoin yarn to 3rd of 8ch, 3dc into first 2ch sp, *into next 2ch sp work [2dc, 3ch, 2dc], 8ch, working backwards 1dc into first of 4dc just worked so making an arch, into arch work [3dc, 3ch, 2dc, 3ch, 2dc, 3ch, 3dc], 3dc into next 2ch sp, rep from * to end. Fasten off.

Simple loop edging Make required number of ch, a multiple of 3 + 8. *Row 1 (RS)* 1tr into 8th ch from hook, *2ch, miss 2ch, 1tr into next ch, rep from * to end. Break off yarn. *Row 2* With RS still facing, rejoin yarn to 3rd of 8ch, *[work 3dc into next 2ch sp] 3 times, 8ch, working backwards miss 5 of dc just worked, ss into 6th dc to make an arch, into arch work [3dc, 3ch, 2dc, 3ch, 2dc, 3ch, 3dc], rep from * to last 2ch sp, 3dc into last 2ch sp. Fasten off.

Irish crochet motifs
Working over a cord
Flower motif

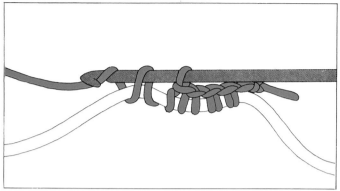

Working over a cord 1. This method gives a firm, slightly ridged, base to the stitches, giving more control to the shape for motifs. Make a slip knot and place on to hook. Holding the cord in the left hand, pass hook under the cord, then wind yarn round hook.

2. Bring loop up in front of cord, then passing hook over the cord, wind yarn round hook and draw through both loops on hook. Continue in this way for required number of double crochet stitches, then gently push all the stitches close together along the cord.

Flower motif 1. *Centre* Make a circle with the cord and work 12dc into it. Pull the 2 ends of the cord to tighten the stitches together. Join the circle with a ss into first dc.

2. *Petals* *Over the cord work 1dc, 12tr, 1dc, tighten the cord, miss 3dc of centre circle, 1ss next dc, rep from * twice more.

3. *Stalk* Work in dc over cord until the stalk is required length. Pull the cord to tighten. Still working over the cord, turn the work and work 1dc into back loop of each dc of stalk, ending with 1ss to edge of petal.

4. *Leaf* Without using the cord, make several chain. Work 1dc into each ch, 3dc into end ch, then 1dc into each ch down second side of chain. Work a second round by working 1htr into each dc, and 3htr at each end.

Simple rose Work the centre as for the flower motif on page 114. Now work 4ch, 1tr into next dc, *1ch, 1tr into next dc, rep from * to end, finishing with 1ss into 3rd of 4ch. Ss into 1ch sp. Working over cord, work 1dc, 5tr, 1dc, miss 2tr, then ss into next 1ch sp of centre. Continue working petals in this way, ending with ss to dc of first petal.

Rose in relief 1. Make centre as for the flower motif on page 114. Now work 6ch, miss next dc, 1tr into next dc, *3ch, miss next dc, 1tr into next dc, rep from * to end, finishing with 1ss into 3rd of 6ch. Into each 3ch sp work [1dc, 3tr, 1dc].

2. *Round 2* Make 2ch, then working behind first round of petals work 1dc at base of 2nd tr of petal, *4ch, 1dc at base of 2nd tr of next petal, rep from * to end. Into each 4ch loop work [1dc, 3tr, 1dc].

3. Continue in this way, working 2 more rounds of petals and working extra chains and trebles to make petals larger as necessary.

Trefoil *Stalk* Work dc tightly over cord to required length. *Leaf* Work in dc over cord for required length of leaf, then still working over cord, work 1dc into base of each dc to end. Do not cut off cord, but work 1 or 2 rounds of dc without cord, ending with ss into last st. Work 2 more leaves in same way, then fasten off.

Bars Worked without cord. Make a loop of chain, then work back in dc. Make a bar of several chain and fix to other side of loop with a ss, turn and work back over it in dc. Continue in this way until required number of bars have been worked. Fasten off.

Hairpin crochet
Double crochet strip
Finishing with double crochet edging
Finishing with crossed loops

Double crochet strip 1. Make a slip knot and place the loop on to the left prong of the hairpin, so that the knot lies in the centre. Wind the yarn round the right prong from front to back. Insert the hook through the loop and catch the yarn.

2. Holding the hairpin in the left hand and the hook in the right hand, draw through a loop, yrh and draw through loop on hook.

3. *Turn the hairpin to the left, allowing the yarn to wind round the prong of the hairpin as you turn it. Insert the hook under the top loop of the left prong, yrh and draw a loop through.

4. Yrh and draw a loop through both loops on hook*. Rep from * to * until the required number of loops have been worked. If there are too many loops on the hairpin, pull the hairpin out and re-insert it through the last 2 or 3 on each side.

Finishing with double crochet edging The simplest way to finish a strip of hairpin crochet, whether it is to be used as a border or an insertion is as follows: join yarn to first loop at one edge, insert hook into loop and work 1ch. Taking care that the loops are not twisted, work 1dc into each loop to end. Fasten off.

Finishing with crossed loops Join yarn to first loop and work 1ch. *Inserting hook from front to back of twisted loop, work 1dc into each of first 6 loops. Insert hook through centre of next 6 loops, then work [2ch, 1dc, 2ch]. Rep from * to end.

Hairpin crochet
Alternative ways of forming strips
Working a circular piece

Some alternative ways of forming the hairpin crochet strips

Strips made with 2 double crochet Work as given for double crochet strips on page 116, working 2dc into front of each loop (see diagram right).

Strips made with 3 double crochet Work as given for double crochet strips, working 3dc into front of each loop.

Strips made with 1dc and 2tr Work as given for double crochet strips, working 1dc and 2tr into front of each loop.

Strips made with groups of stitches Work as given for double crochet strips, working round each loop as follows: yrh 3 times, insert hook under loop on left prong of hairpin, yrh and draw loop through, yrh and draw through all 5 loops on hook.

Strips made with double crochet and closed loops Work as given for double crochet strips, inserting hook below each loop on left prong instead of through it.

Strips made with trebles and closed loops Work as given for double crochet strips, working 1tr round each loop and inserting hook below each loop on left prong instead of through it.

Working a circular piece of hairpin crochet 1. Make a strip of hairpin crochet and remove hairpin, but do not cut off yarn. Thread a spare length of matching yarn through all the loops on one edge, taking care that the loops are all twisted the same way, then draw up tightly and secure.

2. Insert hook back into last stitch from last loop and join to first stitch with a slipstitch. Finish the outer edge by working 1dc into each loop, working 1 or 2 chain between each loop as required.

Joining 2 strips by weaving Lay the 2 strips edge to edge, with the right sides facing upwards. Insert hook through first loop in top strip, then through first loop in bottom strip, draw second loop through first loop. *Insert hook through next loop in top strip and draw through loop on hook, insert hook through next loop in bottom strip and draw through loop on hook, rep from * to end. Fasten off.

Joining 2 strips with chain stitch Lay the 2 strips edge to edge, with the right sides facing upwards. Join yarn to first loop in top strip, insert hook through first loop in top strip, then through first loop in bottom strip, yrh and draw through a loop, yrh and draw through loop on hook, *insert hook through next loop in top strip, then through next loop in bottom strip, yrh and draw through a loop, yrh and draw through loop on hook, rep from * to end. Fasten off.

Joining 2 strips with zigzag chain stitch Lay the 2 strips edge to edge, with the right sides facing upwards. Join yarn to first loop in top strip, insert hook through first loop in top strip, yrh and draw through a loop, yrh and draw through loop on hook, insert hook through first loop in bottom strip, yrh and draw through a loop, yrh and draw through loop on hook, *insert hook through next loop in top strip, yrh and draw through a loop, yrh and draw through loop on hook, insert hook through next loop in bottom strip, yrh and draw through a loop, yrh and draw through loop on hook, rep from * to end. Fasten off.

Joining 2 strips by weaving groups of stitches Lay the 2 strips edge to edge, with the right sides facing upwards. Insert hook through first 2 or 3 loops in top strip, then through same number of loops in bottom strip, draw second group of loops through first group. *Insert hook through next group of loops in top strip and draw through loops on hook, insert hook through next group of loops in bottom strip and draw through loops on hook, rep from * to end. Fasten off.

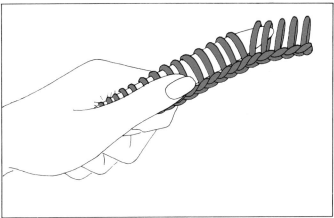

Peruvian crochet 1. This stitch is worked by using one large knitting needle and a hook. Each row is made up of two parts – a forward and a return row, each worked with the right side facing. Commence with the required number of chain, which in this example is divisible by 5. On the forward row begin by placing the first chain loop on to the needle. *Insert the hook through the next ch, yrh, draw a loop through and place on to the needle.

2. Holding the needle in the left hand, rep from * to end of chain, taking care to keep all loops the same length. Note that this row forms the foundation row for the work.

3. Working from right to left and holding the needle in the left hand and the hook in the right hand, insert the hook through the first 5 loops, yrh and draw through a loop, yrh and draw through loop on hook. Now working through all 5 loops again, work 5dc, *inserting hook through the centre of the next 5 loops, work 5dc, rep from * to end.

4. Working from left to right and holding the needle in the left hand and the hook in the right hand, insert the hook into the first dc, yrh, draw a loop through and place on to the needle. *Insert the hook into the next dc, yrh, draw a loop through and place on to the needle, rep from * to end. Repeat steps 3 and 4 to form pattern, ending with row 3.

Simple Tunisian stitch 1. This stitch is worked with a special Tunisian crochet hook on a base of ch stitch. *Row 1 (forward)* Insert hook into 2nd ch from hook, yrh, draw loop through and leave on hook, *insert hook through next ch, yrh, draw through loop and leave on hook, rep from * to end. Do not turn the work.

2. *Row 1 (return)* Still with right side of work facing, work yrh, draw through first loop on hook, *yrh, draw through 2 loops on hook, rep from * to end. This completes the 2 sections of the first row.

3. *Row 2 (forward)* Insert hook from right to left under 2nd vertical loop of last row, yrh, draw loop through, *insert hook under next vertical loop, yrh, draw loop through, rep from * to end.

4. Work the *return row* as given for row 1, then repeat row 2 (forward and return) to form pattern. This stitch forms the basic technique for simple Tunisian stitch patterns.

Double Tunisian stitch Make req no of ch and work *row 1* as simple Tunisian st. *Row 2 (forward)* Yrh, draw through lp on hook, *insert hook through next vertical lp of prev row, yrh, draw lp through, yrh, draw through lp on hook, rep from * to end. Work return row as simple Tunisian st; rep row 2 to form patt.

Finishing the work Although the work seems finished at the end of a return row, the edge can be a bit ragged and tends to 'curl'. To give a neat edge, work 1 row of dc, inserting hook under vertical loop of each stitch and completing each stitch as it is worked.

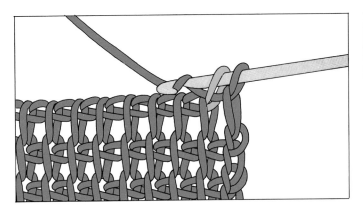

Increasing a stitch at the edge of a row A stitch can be increased at either end of the row, but it must be worked on the forward row. At the beginning of the row, work the first stitch, then insert hook through horizontal stitch between first and 2nd stitches and draw a loop through. Work in same way at end of row.

Increasing more than 1 stitch at the beginning of a row Make the same number of chain as the required number of increased stitches, then work these stitches in the normal way.

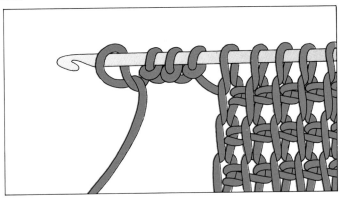

Increasing more than 1 stitch at the end of a row Work to end of a forward row, then make extra stitches by forming a loop in the yarn, twisting it to place on hook. Tighten the stitch, then form the next one until the required number of stitches has been increased. Work these stitches off in the normal way.

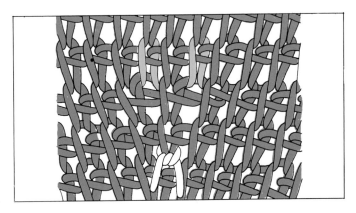

Increasing in the middle of a row Mark the position for the increased stitches. Work to the position of the increase, then make an extra stitch by inserting the hook under the horizontal thread between the stitches and drawing a loop through.

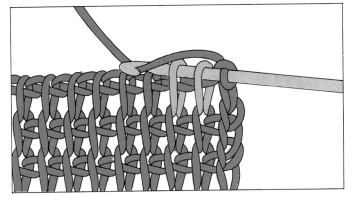

Decreasing at the edge of a row If decrease is at beginning work the first stitch normally, then insert hook through next 2 vertical loops together and draw through only 1 loop. If it is at the end work to last 3 stitches, work 2 together, then work last stitch.

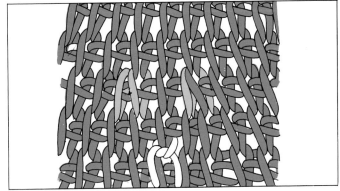

Decreasing in the middle of a row Mark the position for the decreased stitches. Work to the position for the decrease, then work the next 2 stitches together as for the decrease at the edge of a row.

Tunisian crochet

Simple Tunisian stitch   Textured rib
Crossed Tunisian stitch   Triple rib
Reverse Tunisian stitch

Simple Tunisian stitch Make required number of ch. *Row 1 (forward)* Insert hook into 2nd ch from hook, yrh, draw loop through and leave on hook, *insert hook through next ch, yrh, draw through loop and leave on hook, rep from * to end. *Row 1 (return)* Yrh, draw through first loop on hook, *yrh, draw through 2 loops on hook, rep from * to end. *Row 2 (forward)* Insert hook through 2nd vertical loop of last row, yrh, draw loop through, *insert hook through next vertical loop, yrh, draw loop through, rep from * to end. *Row 2 (return)* Yrh, draw through first loop on hook, *yrh, draw through 2 loops on hook, rep from * to end. Rep row 2 (forward and return) to form patt.

Reverse Tunisian stitch Make required number of ch. Work *row 1 (forward and return rows)* as given for simple Tunisian stitch. *Row 2 (forward)* With yarn at front of work, insert hook through 2nd vertical loop of last row, yrh from back to front, draw through a loop and leave on hook, *ytf, insert hook through next vertical loop, yrh from back to front, draw through loop, rep from * to end. *Row 2 (return)* Yrh, draw through first loop on hook, *yrh, draw through 2 loops on hook, rep from * to end. Rep row 2 (forward and return) to form patt.

Crossed Tunisian stitch Make required number of ch, a multiple of 2 + 1. Work *Row 1 (forward and return rows)* as given for simple Tunisian stitch. *Row 2 (forward)* Insert hook under vertical loop of 3rd st, yrh, draw loop through, passing hook back across front of work, insert through vertical loop of 2nd st, yrh, draw loop through, *miss next loop, insert hook under next loop, yrh, draw loop through, passing hook back across in front of work, insert under missed loop, yrh and draw loop through, rep from * to end. *Row 2 (return)* Yrh, draw through first loop on hook, *yrh, draw through 2 loops on hook, rep from * to end. *Row 3 (forward)* Insert hook through 2nd vertical loop of last row, yrh, draw loop through, *insert hook through next vertical loop, yrh, draw loop through, rep from * to end. *Row 3 (return)* Yrh, draw through first loop on hook, *yrh, draw through 2 loops on hook, rep from * to end. Rep rows 2 and 3 (forward and return) to form patt.

Textured rib Make required number of ch, a multiple of 2 + 1. Work *row 1 (forward and return rows)* as given for simple Tunisian stitch. *Row 2 (forward)* Miss the first st, insert hook under 2nd vertical loop, yrh and draw loop through, *yrh twice, insert hook through next 2 vertical loops tog, yrh and draw loop through, yrh and draw through 2 loops on hook, rep from * to last st, insert hook under last st, yrh and draw loop through. *Row 2 (return)* Yrh, draw through first loop on hook, *yrh, draw through 2 loops on hook, rep from * to end. Rep row 2 (forward and return) to form patt.

Triple rib Make required number of ch, a multiple of 6 + 1. Work *row 1 (forward and return rows)* as given for simple Tunisian stitch. *Row 2 (forward)* Work alternately 3 simple Tunisian stitches, then 3 reverse Tunisian stitches to end of row. *Row 2 (return)* Yrh, draw through first loop on hook, *yrh, draw through 2 loops on hook, rep from * to end. Rep row 2 (forward and return) to form patt.

Butterfly stitch Make required number of ch, a multiple of 10 + 6. Work *row 1 (forward and return rows)* as given for simple Tunisian stitch. *Rows 2 to 5* Work as simple Tunisian stitch. *Row 6 (forward)* *Work 5sT, (insert hook through centre of st 4 rows below 3rd st to left, draw a long loop through, insert hook back into next vertical loop of row 5, yrh and draw through a long loop on hook – called Loop 1), [work 1sT, then Loop 1 through same st as before] twice, rep from * to last 5 sts, work 5sT. *Row 6 (return)* Yrh, draw through first loop on hook, *yrh, draw through 2 loops on hook, rep from * to end. *Rows 7 to 10* Work 5 rows simple Tunisian st. *Row 11 (forward)* Work 3sT, *[Loop 1, 1sT] twice, Loop 1, work 5sT, rep from * to last 2 sts, work 2sT. *Row 11 (return)* Yrh, draw through first loop on hook, *yrh, draw through 2 loops on hook, rep from * to end. Rep rows 2 to 11 (forward and return) to form patt.

Scattered eyelet stitch Make required number of ch, a multiple of 6 + 4. Work *row 1 (forward and return rows)* as given for simple Tunisian stitch. *Row 2 (forward)* Miss first st, [insert hook under vertical loop of next st, yrh and draw loop through] 3 times, *yrh twice, miss next 2 sts, [insert hook under vertical loop of next st, yrh and draw loop through] 4 times, rep from * to end. *Row 2 and all return rows (return)* Yrh, draw through first loop on hook, *yrh, draw through 2 loops on hook, rep from * to end. *Row 3 (forward)* Work in simple Tunisian st. *Row 4 (forward)* Miss first st, insert hook under vertical loop of next st, yrh and draw loop through, *yrh twice, miss next 2 sts, [insert hook under vertical loop of next st, yrh and draw loop through] 4 times, rep from * to last 6 sts, yrh twice, miss next 2 sts, [insert hook under vertical loop of next st, yrh and draw loop through] twice. *Row 5 (forward)* Work in simple Tunisian st. Rep rows 2 to 5 (forward) and return) to form patt.

Diagonal stitch Make required number of ch, a multiple of 5. Work *row 1 (forward and return rows)* as given for simple Tunisian stitch. *Row 2 (forward)* *Work 4sT (simple Tunisian), 1rT (reverse Tunisian), rep from * to end. *Row 2 and all return rows (return):* Yrh, draw through first loop on hook, *yrh, draw through 2 loops on hook, rep from * to end. *Row 3* 3sT, *1rT, 4sT, rep from * to last 2 sts, 1rT, 1sT. *Row 4* 2sT, *1rT, 4sT, rep from * to last 3 sts, 1rT, 2sT. *Row 5* 1sT, *1rT, 4sT, rep from * to last 4 sts, 1rT, 3sT. *Row 6* *1rT, 4sT, rep from * to end. Rep rows 2 to 6 (forward and return) to form patt.

Mesh stitch Make required number of ch, a multiple of 2 + 1. *Row 1 (forward)* *Yrh, miss next ch, draw loop through next ch, rep from * to end. *Row 1 and all return rows (return)* Yrh, draw through first loop on hook, *yrh, draw through 2 loops on hook, rep from * to end. *Row 2 (forward)* *Yrh, insert hook through vertical loop of next st, yrh and draw loop through, rep from * to end. Rep row 2 (forward and return) to form patt.

Tunisian crochet

Simple grain of rice stitch Double grain of rice stitch
Horizontal ridge stitch Full Tunisian stitch
Tunisian stocking stitch

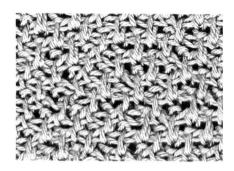

Simple grain of rice stitch Make required number of ch, a multiple of 2 + 1. Work *row 1 (forward and return rows)* as given for simple Tunisian stitch. *Row 2 (forward)* *Work 1sT, 1rT, rep from * to end. *Row 2 (return)* Yrh, draw through first loop on hook, *yrh, draw through 2 loops on hook, rep from * to end. *Row 3 (forward)* *Work 1rT, 1sT, rep from * to end. *Row 3 (return)* Yrh, draw through first loop on hook, *yrh, draw through 2 loops on hook, rep from * to end. Rep rows 2 and 3 to form patt.

Horizontal ridge stitch Make required number of ch. Work *row 1 (forward and return rows)* as given for simple Tunisian stitch. *Row 2 (forward)* 1ch, *yrh, insert hook under vertical loop of next st, yrh and draw through loop, yrh and draw through first 2 loops on hook, rep from * to end. *Row 2 (return)* Yrh, draw through first loop on hook, *yrh, draw through 2 loops on hook, rep from * to end. *Row 3 (forward)* Work 1 row simple Tunisian st. *Row 3 (return)* Yrh, draw through first loop on hook, *yrh, draw through 2 loops on hook, rep from * to end. *Row 4 (forward)* *Insert hook below vertical loop of next st, yrh and draw through a loop, rep from * to end. *Row 4 (return)* Yrh, draw through first loop on hook, *yrh, draw through 2 loops on hook, rep from * to end. Rep rows 2 to 4 (forward and return) to form patt.

NOTE A Tunisian treble (Ttr) is worked as given for *Row 2 (forward)* in Horizontal ridge stitch (above), beginning at the asterisk.

Double grain of rice stitch Make required number of ch, a multiple of 4 + 1. Work *row 1 (forward and return rows)* as given for simple Tunisian stitch. *Row 2 (forward)* *Work 2sT, 2rT, rep from * to end. *Row 2 (return)* Yrh, draw through first loop on hook, *yrh, draw through 2 loops on hook, rep from * to end. *Row 3 (forward)* *Work 2rT, 2sT, rep from * to end. *Row 3 (return)* Yrh, draw through first loop on hook, *yrh, draw through 2 loops on hook, rep from * to end. Rep row 2 (forward and return) to form patt.

Tunisian stocking stitch Make required number of ch. Work *row 1 (forward and return rows)* as given for simple Tunisian stitch. *Row 2 (forward)* *Insert hook from front to back through centre of next st (between the 2 vertical loops), yrh and draw loop through, rep from * to end. *Row 2 (return)* Yrh, draw through first loop on hook, *yrh, draw through 2 loops on hook, rep from * to end. Rep row 2 (forward and return) to form patt.

Full Tunisian stitch Make required number of ch. Work *row 1 (forward and return rows)* as given for simple Tunisian stitch. *Row 2 (forward)* *Insert hook under horizontal thread between next 2 vertical loops, yrh and draw loop through, rep from * to end, work last st into end vertical loop. *Row 2 (return)* Yrh, draw through first loop on hook, *yrh, draw through 2 loops on hook, rep from * to end. Rep row 2 (forward and return) to form patt.

Tunisian crochet

Slanting rib   English rib
Open fan stitch   Granite stitch
                Cable pattern

Slanting rib   Make required number of ch, a multiple of 6 + 1. Work *row 1 (forward and return rows)* as given for simple Tunisian stitch. *Row 2 (forward)* *Work 3sT, 3rT, rep from * to end. *Row 2 (return)* Yrh, draw through first loop on hook, *yrh, draw through 2 loops on hook, rep from * to end. *Row 3 (forward)* Work 1rT, *3sT, 2rT, rep from * to last 5 sts, work 3sT, 2rT. *Row 3 (return)* Yrh, draw through first loop on hook, *yrh, draw through 2 loops on hook, rep from * to end. Continue working in this way, moving the patt over 1 st on every row to form diagonal patt.

Open fan stitch   Make required number of ch, a multiple of 4 + 1. Work *row 1 (forward)* as given for simple Tunisian stitch. *Row 1 (return)* *3ch, yrh and draw loop through first st on hook, yrh, draw through 4 loops on hook, rep from * to end. *Row 2 (forward)* *Insert hook into top of 4 st group, yrh and draw loop through [yrh and draw loop through next ch] 3 times, rep from * to end. *Row 2 (return)* Yrh, draw through first loop on hook, *yrh, draw through 2 loops on hook, rep from * to end. Rep row 2 (forward and return) to form patt.

Granite stitch   Make required number of ch, a multiple of 4 + 1. Work *row 1 (forward and return rows)* as given for simple Tunisian stitch. *Row 2 (forward)* *Work 2sT, 2rT, rep from * to end. *Row 2 (return)* Yrh, draw through first loop on hook, *yrh, draw through 2 loops on hook, rep from * to end. *Row 3 (forward)* Work in simple Tunisian st. *Row 3 (return)* Yrh, draw through first loop on hook, *yrh, draw through 2 loops on hook, rep from * to end. *Row 4 (forward)* *Work 2rT, 2Ttr, rep from * to end. *Row 4 (return)* Yrh, draw through first loop on hook, *yrh, draw through 2 loops on hook, rep from * to end. *Row 5 (forward)* Work in simple Tunisian st. *Row 5 (return)* Yrh, draw through first loop on hook, *yrh, draw through 2 loops on hook, rep from * to end. *Row 6 (forward)* *Work 2Ttr, 2rT, rep from * to end. *Row 6 (return)* Yrh, draw through first loop on hook, * yrh, draw through 2 loops on hook, rep from * to end. Rep rows 3 to 6 (forward and return) to form patt.

English rib   Make required number of ch, a multiple of 4 + 1. Work *row 1 (forward and return rows)* as given for simple Tunisian stitch. *Row 2 (forward)* *Work 2sT, 2rT, rep from * to end. *Row 2 (return)* Yrh, draw through first loop on hook, *yrh, draw through 2 loops on hook, rep from * to end. Rep row 2 (forward and return) to form patt.

Cable pattern   Make required number of ch, a multiple of 6 + 1. *Row 1 (forward)* *Work 4sT, 2rT, rep from * to end. *Row 1 (return)* Yrh, draw through first loop on hook, *yrh, draw through 2 loops on hook, rep from * to end. *Rows 2 to 4 (forward and return)* As row 1. *Row 5 (forward)* *Miss next 2sT sts, work 1sT into each of next 2sT sts, crossing in front of last 2sts work 1sT into each of the 2 missed sT sts, work 2rT, rep from * to end. *Row 5 (return)* Yrh, draw through first loop on hook, *yrh, draw through 2 loops on hook, rep from * to end. *Row 6 (forward and return)* As row 1. Rep rows 1 to 6 (forward and return) to form patt.

Tunisian crochet

Natalie stitch   Laura stitch
Julia stitch   Erica stitch

Natalie stitch In A make required number of ch, a multiple of 10 + 2. Work *row 1 (forward and return rows)* in A, as given for simple Tunisian stitch. *Row 2 (forward)* In B, work 1Tss (insert hook through next loop but do not draw loop through), *work 2sT, 4Ttr, 2sT, 2Tss, rep from * to end. *Row 2 (return)* In B, yrh, draw through first loop on hook, *yrh, draw through 2 loops on hook, rep from * to end. *Row 3 (forward)* In A, work in simple Tunisian st. *Row 3 (return)* In A, yrh, draw through first loop on hook, *yrh, draw through 2 loops on hook, rep from * to end. *Row 4 (forward)* In B, work 2Ttr, *work 2sT, 2Tss, 2sT, 4Ttr, rep from * to end. *Row 4 (return)* In B, yrh, draw through first loop on hook, *yrh, draw through 2 loops on hook, rep from * to end. *Row 5 (forward)* In A, work in simple Tunisian st. *Row 5 (return)* In A, yrh, draw through first loop on hook, *yrh, draw through 2 loops on hook, rep from * to end. Rep rows 1 to 5 (forward and return) to form patt.

Laura stitch In A make required number of ch, a multiple of 4 + 1. Work *row 1 (forward and return rows)* in A, as given for simple Tunisian stitch. *Row 2 (forward and return)* In A, work in simple Tunisian st. *Row 3 (forward)* In B, *insert hook through vertical loops of next 3 sts, yrh and draw through a loop, then working into the 3rd of the 3 loops only work 1sT and 1rT, 1sT into next loop, rep from * to end. *Row 3 (return)* In B, yrh, draw through first loop on hook, *yrh, draw through 2 loops on hook, rep from * to end. Rep rows 2 and 3 (forward and return) to form patt.

Julia stitch In A make required number of ch, a multiple of 6 + 1. Work *row 1 (forward and return rows)* in A, as given for simple Tunisian stitch. *Row 2 (forward)* In B, *work 3Ttr, 3sT, rep from * to end. *Row 2 (return)* In B, yrh, draw through first loop on hook, *yrh, draw through 2 loops on hook, rep from * to end. *Row 3 (forward)* In A, *work 3sT, 3Ttr, rep from * to end. *Row 3 (return)* In A, yrh, draw through first loop on hook, *yrh, draw through 2 loops on hook, rep from * to end. Rep rows 2 and 3 (forward and return) to form patt.

Erica stitch In A make required number of ch, a multiple of 4 + 1. *Row 1 (forward)* In A, *work 2sT, 2rT, rep from * to end. *Row 1 (return)* In A, yrh, draw through first loop on hook, *yrh, draw through 2 loops on hook, rep from * to end. *Row 2 (forward)* In B, *work 2rT, 2sT, rep from * to end. *Row 2 (return)* In B, yrh, draw through first loop on hook, *yrh, draw through 2 loops on hook, rep from * to end. Rep rows 2 and 3 (forward and return) to form patt.

Nicola stitch In A make required number of ch, a multiple of 2 + 1. Work *row 1 (forward and return rows)* in A, as given for simple Tunisian stitch. *Row 2 (forward)* In A, *insert hook through next 2 vertical loops, yrh and draw loop through, insert hook into horizontal bar before next vertical loop, yrh and draw loop through, rep from * to end. *Row 2 (return)* In B, yrh, draw through first loop on hook, *yrh, draw through 2 loops on hook, rep from * to end. *Row 3 (forward)* In B, work as given for row 2. *Row 3 (return)* In C, yrh, draw through first loop on hook, *yrh, draw through 2 loops on hook, rep from * to end. *Row 4 (forward)* In C, work as given for row 2. *Row 4 (return)* In A, yrh, draw through first loop on hook, *yrh, draw through 2 loops on hook, rep from * to end. Rep rows 2 to 4 (forward and return) to form patt.

Anna stitch In A make required number of ch, a multiple of 2 + 1. Work *row 1 (forward and return rows)* in A, as given for simple Tunisian stitch. *Row 2 (forward)* In B, *miss next loop, work 1sT into next loop, rep from * to end. *Row 2 (return)* In B, yrh, draw through 1 loop, *1ch, yrh, draw through next 2 loops on hook, rep from * to last st, yrh and draw through last 2 loops. *Row 3 (forward)* In C, *1sT into next loop, 1Ttr into 1ch sp, rep from * to last st, 1sT into last st. *Row 3 (return)* In C, yrh, draw through first loop on hook, *yrh, draw through 2 loops on hook, rep from * to end. *Row 4 (forward)* In A, 1sT into next loop, *insert hook through vertical loops of sT and Ttr, yrh and draw through loop, rep from * to end. *Row 4 (return)* In A, yrh and draw loop through 1 loop, *1ch, yrh and draw through 2 loops, rep from * to last st, yrh and draw through last 2 loops. Rep rows 2 to 4 (forward and return) to form patt.

Gwendoline stitch In A make required number of ch, a multiple of 2 + 3. Work *row 1 (forward and return rows)* in A, as given for simple Tunisian stitch. *Row 2 (forward)* In B, *yrh, insert hook through next 2 vertical loops, yrh and draw through loop, rep from * to last 2 sts, 1sT into each of last 2 loops. *Row 2 (return)* In C, yrh, draw through first loop on hook, *yrh, draw through 2 loops on hook, rep from * to end. *Row 3 (forward)* In C, work as given for row 2. *Row 3 (return)* In A, yrh, draw through first loop on hook, *yrh, draw through 2 loops on hook, rep from * to end. *Row 4 (forward)* In A, work as given for row 2. *Row 4 (return)* In B, yrh, draw through first loop on hook, *yrh, draw through 2 loops on hook, rep from * to end. Rep rows 2 to 4 (forward and return) to form patt.

Victoria stitch In A make required number of ch, a multiple of 3. Work *row 1 (forward and return rows)* in A, as given for simple Tunisian stitch. *Row 2 (forward)* In B, *work 2sT, miss next loop, rep from * to last 2 loops, work 2sT. *Row 2 (return)* In B, yrh and draw through 1 loop, yrh and draw through 2 loops, 1ch, *[yrh and draw through 2 loops] twice, 1ch, rep from * to last 3 sts, [yrh and draw through 2 loops] 3 times. *Row 3 (forward and return)* In C, work as given for row 2. *Row 4 (forward)* In A, *work 2sT, 1Ttr into ch loop, rep from * to last 2 sts, 2sT. *Row 4 (return)* In A, yrh, draw through first loop on hook, *yrh, draw through 2 loops on hook, rep from * to end. Rep rows 2 to 4 (forward and return) to form patt.

INTRODUCTION
TO
EMBROIDERY & NEEDLEPOINT

This section introduces the fascinating craft of embroidery with a wide selection of beautiful stitches and techniques for decorative or practical purposes. It explains the basics of drawn thread work, smocking, appliqué and needlepoint to name just a few, and provides an invaluable stitch reference for those working their own designs.

Embroidery is an exciting field to explore because of its sheer versatility. Depending on the technique and on the fabric and thread chosen, the result can be as delicate as a lacy tablecloth or as bold as a colourful wall hanging. It can be put to a practical purpose such as a hard-wearing needlepoint chair seat cover or it can be purely decorative, to enhance a collar or a child's dress for example.

The range of fabrics, threads and needles is extensive and it is important to use the correct combination for the results you want to achieve.

Fabrics Some embroidery stitches can be worked on practically any fabric from fine linen and cotton to silk, tulle, velvet and even felt. Certain techniques, however, have more specific requirements. Counted thread and drawn thread work must be done on an evenweave fabric, which has an equal number of warp and weft threads over a square area.

Needlepoint is worked on canvas which is a firm material woven with either single or double threads. The number of threads (or double threads) to 2.5cm (1in) varies from coarse rug canvas with $3\frac{1}{3}$ threads to 2.5cm (1in) to fine canvas with 26 threads to 2.5cm (1in). Most needlepoint, however, is worked on canvas in the range of 12 to 20 threads to 2.5cm (1in). Plastic canvas is

also available and, being more rigid, is useful for bags or boxes which do not then need to be backed.

Threads Some embroidery techniques require certain types of thread, whereas with others you can experiment to achieve different effects. Stranded cotton, pearl cotton and coton à broder are all shiny threads which can be used for free embroidery and for counted thread work. Stranded cotton is useful as it can be separated into six strands which can then be combined to achieve different thicknesses. Soft embroidery cotton is a matt cotton thread also suitable for free embroidery.

Woollen threads include crewel wool, tapestry wool and rug wool. Although needlepoint traditionally uses woollen threads, any embroidery thread can be used for special effects, including knitting yarns and even fine ribbon.

For sumptuous work such as gold work, there is a variety of metallic and silk threads available, including pure gold.

Needles It is important to use the correct needle for the type of embroidery you are working. The needle should be large enough to carry the thread through the fabric easily without distorting the woven threads.

All types of needles come in a range of sizes. Crewel and chenille needles have a sharp point and a large eye suitable for holding a variety of embroidery threads. For counted thread work and needlepoint, tapestry needles with blunt ends are necessary in order not to split the fabric threads. For sewing on beads, a special fine beading needle is required.

Frames Although some embroidery can be worked in the hand, the finished result is more satisfactory, with neater stitches, if the fabric is stretched in a frame. Ring frames are versatile and easy to use for embroidery. Different types are available – some can be hand-held, others clamped to a table or fixed to a floor stand. They consist of an inner ring and an adjustable outer ring which is tightened by means of a screw. Before using a ring frame, bind the inner ring with bias binding to protect the fabric.

Canvas may be mounted on a rectangular slate frame which has two cross bars and two side bars and is available in different sizes. It is tightened either by a screw method or by positioning pegs in peg holes, and can be held in the hand or mounted on a stand. Alternatively the fabric or canvas can simply be stretched over a plain wooden frame and tacked or stapled down.

Running and Back stitches
Running stitch   Back stitch
Back stitch and Seeding   Double back stitch

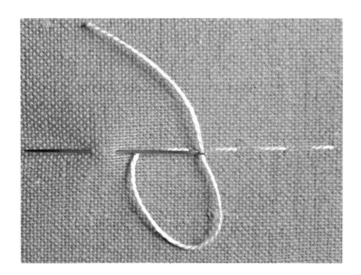

Running stitch Some embroidery stitches are used to outline motifs in a design. They can also be used in a decorative border. The easiest of these stitches, also used in plain sewing, is running stitch. Work from right to left in a straight line. The needle passes in and out of the fabric making a row of evenly spaced, even-sized stitches.

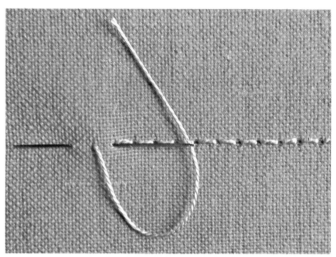

Back stitch 1 This stitch is also frequently used in plain sewing. In embroidery, it is mainly used to make an outline, or as a base line for other decorative stitches. One variation is to weave a thread of a different colour through the stitches. Working from right to left, bring the needle through to the right side of the fabric and make a small backward stitch. Bring the needle out the same number of threads to the left. Continue in this way, always returning to the end of the previous stitch.

Back stitch 2 and Seeding Use a stepped back stitch to create geometric shapes with even-sized stitches. Small separate back stitches can be used to fill spaces, giving the effect of scattered small dots. To make them more obvious go over each stitch twice, doubling them. This technique is called seeding.

Double back stitch Working from right to left, make a back stitch over three threads, bringing the needle out at the starting point. Work a second stitch over the first, bringing the needle out three threads to the left. Pull all stitches firmly. Continue in this way, forming a type of reinforced back stitch and pulled threads. This resembles a stitch used in drawn fabric work. It is the main variation of back stitch and is most often used for finishing off household linen such as tablecloths.

Stem stitches

Stem stitch   Threaded stem stitch
Alternating stem stitch   Darned stem stitch
Cable stem stitch   Whipped stem stitch

Stem stitch This is a widely used stitch as it is complementary to satin stitch and other filling stitches and is good for outlining and making curving lines. Working from left to right, pass the needle to the left under two or three threads of the fabric. Move along the line of the design to the right and make a second stitch to the left, picking up the same number of threads. The needle always emerges just above the previous stitch, giving the effect of a fine twisted cord.

Threaded stem stitch Work a row of ordinary stem stitch, then with a thread of a contrasting colour, weave in and out of the stitches. Start by passing the thread under the first stitch from the top, and then under the second stitch from the bottom. Use a fine thread for the stem stitch and a thicker one for the undulating threading.

Darned stem stitch Sew three of more rows of ordinary stem stitch, one under the other. Then pass another thread up and down under alternate stitches. To achieve a relief effect, use threads of both different colour and thickness.

Alternating stem stitch Make a row of stem stitch with the needle emerging alternately above and below the previous stitch, giving a different effect from the twisted cord. Use a long stitch and a thick thread for a relief effect.

Cable stem stitch Make two rows of alternating stem stitch, so that the stitches lie together or apart alternately, giving a chain effect. This makes a pleasing border, and can also be worked in curves.

Whipped stem stitch Work a row of stem stitch using fairly long stitches. Then using a thread of a contrasting colour, pass the needle through each stitch without going through the fabric. Work from left to right.

Curving whipped stem stitch Work a row of curving stem stitch, keeping the stitches diagonal by inserting the needle slightly lower with each stitch on a downward curve and the reverse on an upward curve. Working from left to right, whip these stitches with a contrasting colour.

Chain stitches

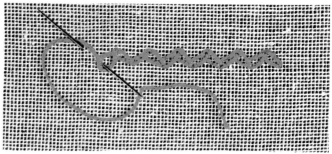

Chain stitch Work from right to left. Bring the needle through to the right side of the fabric. Stitch into the same point, picking up several threads of the fabric, and loop the embroidery thread round the emerging point of the needle. Pull the needle through and make a second stitch, again catching the loop. Keep the stitches fairly loose.

Zigzag chain stitch Work from right to left. Work simple chain stitches diagonally, one upwards and one downwards alternately. Make them of regular size and spacing.

Sloping chain stitch Working in a straight line, bring the thread through to the right side of the fabric. Stitch not into the same point, but several threads of the fabric to the left, leaving a loop. Bring the needle out diagonally downwards, and wind the loop round the tip of the needle before pulling the thread through. Catch the loop with a small oblique stitch.

Open chain stitch Work from right to left. This is similar to ordinary chain stitch, but instead of making the next stitch by stitching back into the same hole, stitch several threads of the fabric lower, inside the loop, slanting the needle up and forwards. Loop the thread round the point of the needle.

Russian chain stitch This is a variation of simple chain stitch. Make an ordinary single chain stitch. Start the second stitch inside the loop, and catch it down with a tiny stitch to one side of the first stitch. Make a third stitch in the same way on the other side. Start a second group of three stitches to the left of the first, and continue to form a row.

Lazy daisy or Detached chain stitch This is similar to Russian chain stitch and is used to make flowers and leaves. First decide how many petals a flower needs and use one chain stitch for each petal, catching it down with a tiny stitch. Work in a circle to complete the flower.

Chain stitches
Cable chain stitch
Interlaced cable chain stitch
Lock stitch

Cable chain stitch This stitch can be worked either as a straight line or in curves. Work vertically, from top to bottom. Bring the thread to the right side of the fabric and make a chain stitch. Place the thread in a left to right loop on the fabric. Pass the needle first under and then over the thread at the top of the loop, making a twist. Then insert the needle into the fabric to make the short linking stitch and bring it out again for the next chain stitch. Make the chain stitches double the length of the stitch in between.

Interlaced cable chain stitch This stitch can be used to cover an area of fabric. Work three or more rows of cable chain stitch, then decorate the rows with a thread of the same or a contrasting colour by lacing through the corresponding loops of the first two rows. Repeat this process with the second and third rows etc, forming a network.

Lock stitch 1. This stitch is made in stages. The foundation, working from right to left, is to make a row of equally sized and spaced vertical stitches. The first stage is worked from left to right, starting at the base of the first stitch. Holding the thread in a loop below the sewing line, thread the needle under the vertical stitch from right to left and pull the thread taut. Work in the same way through the next vertical stitch, but with the thread held in a loop above the stitching. Continue to the end of the row.

2. Work from right to left in the second stage of the stitch. Repeat the previous stage in reverse, without turning the work.

Buttonhole and Blanket stitches

Blanket stitch   Cording
Buttonhole stitch   Padded scallop stitch
Scallop stitch

Blanket stitch and Buttonhole stitch These stitches are made in the same way, but blanket stitch is more widely spaced than buttonhole stitch. Working from left to right, bring the thread through to the right side of the fabric on the base line. Make a loop with the thread and hold it in position with the thumb. Stitch from above, and downwards to the base line. Pull the thread through, tightening the loop.

Cording Working in two stages, first make a row of running stitches as a guide line and lay a thicker thread alongside as a filling. Then complete the cording by stitching over the running stitches and filling thread with small, very close, vertical stitches, so that they are completely covered.

Scallop stitch This stitch is used to give a finishing touch to the edge of a piece of work. Make a straight line of running stitches, and placing a button on the line, mark round it to give regular scallop shapes. Working over this guide line, use short, close buttonhole stitches to outline the shapes. Cut off the excess fabric very carefully.

Padded scallop stitch This is used in scallop-shaped patterns. Mark out the scallops on the right side of the fabric and fill them with rows of running stitch to make a filling for the completed shape. With buttonhole stitches of varying lengths, cover the shapes exactly.

Buttonhole and Blanket stitches

Closed blanket stitch   Two colour blanket stitch
Boat stitch   Loop stitch
Crossed blanket stitch   Woven blanket stitch

Closed blanket stitch Blanket stitches can add a decorative element to a ready folded and tacked hem, and can be used instead of ordinary hemming. Closed blanket stitch is worked from left to right. Bring the thread through to the right side of the fabric at the hem edge and stitch up to the right. Come out again down to the left. Go in at the top of the stitch again and stitch down to the right. Repeat these two stitches, keeping the thread under the needle.

Two colour blanket stitch This is two rows of blanket stitch, one over the other. Sew the first row in one colour keeping the stitches about 5mm ($\frac{3}{16}$in) apart. With the second colour work along the same row, between the existing stitches, but using shorter stitches. The same method can be used with more than two colours by making the distance between each colour greater.

Boat stitch The sails of the boat are made by working three blanket stitches into the same starting point. The boat itself is made with straight stitches.

Crossed blanket stitch Bring the thread through to the right side of the work and stitch diagonally to the right. The next stitch, which is diagonally to the left, starts to the left of the first stitch with the needle emerging to the right. Keep the thread held under the needle.

Loop stitch Working from right to left, bring the needle up at the centre line. Insert it up and to the left, and bring out vertically below. Pass the needle under the previous stitch as shown.

Woven blanket stitch Make a row of blanket stitch with closely-worked long stitches. Using the same colour or a contrasting one, darn rows of threads over and under the blanket stitch to give a woven effect.

Feather stitches

Feather stitch   Straight feather stitch   Double feather stitch   Fly stitch
Single feather stitch   Closed feather stitch   Triple feather stitch   Arrow stitch

Feather stitch Working from top to bottom, pick up several threads of the fabric to the left, holding the needle obliquely and stitching towards the centre with the thread under the needle. Repeat this to the right and continue in the same way.

Single feather stitch This is done in the same way as feather stitch, but working only to one side, left or right, holding the thread at the centre. It gives the effect of sloping blanket stitch.

Double feather stitch Work as for feather stitch, making alternately two stitches to the left and two to the right, giving the effect of a sloping, alternating blanket stitch.

Triple feather stitch This is done in the same way as double feather stitch, but working three stitches to the left and three to the right, instead of two.

Straight feather stitch This is worked in the same way as feather stitch, but holding the needle vertically when making the left and right-hand stitches.

Closed feather stitch This is worked in the same way as straight feather stitch, but without leaving spaces between the stitches. It can be used on drawn thread work.

Fly stitch Working from left to right, bring the needle out at the left, insert again several threads to the right and out at the bottom centre of the stitch, keeping the thread under the needle. Finish with a small stitch to hold.

Arrow stitch This is a variation of fly stitch. Make a fly stitch, catching the thread at the centre, and stitching up and out again, finishing at bottom centre.

Knotted stitches

Coral stitch   Zigzag coral stitch
French knots   Knotted buttonhole stitch
Scroll stitch   Bullion stitch

Coral stitch (left) This stitch is worked from right to left. Bring the thread through to the right side of the fabric, then make a small vertical stitch a little to the left, making sure that the thread passes under the point of the needle from left to right. Pull gently to the left to form a knot.

Zigzag coral stitch (right) Proceed as for the previous stitch, working the stitches one upwards and one downwards, making a zigzag pattern. When tightening the stitch, always hold the thread in the direction of the next stitch, alternately up and down.

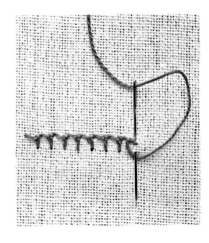

French knots (left) Bring the thread through to the right side of the fabric. Take a tiny diagonal stitch, without pulling the needle through. Wind the thread round the needle two or three times and draw the needle through the knot. Stitch back into the fabric near the starting point, pulling the knot tight.

Knotted buttonhole stitch (right) Work from left to right. Bring the needle through to the right side of the fabric and pick up one thread of the fabric to the right, passing the needle through the loop. Tighten the stitch. Make a second stitch over the first, picking up more threads.

Scroll stitch (left) Work from right to left. Bring the needle through to the right side of the fabric, loop the thread as shown and stitch obliquely downwards, picking up one or two threads inside the loop. Draw the thread through to the left, without making the stitches too tight.

Bullion stitch (right) Make a back stitch, the size of the bullion stitch required, and bring the needle point out where it first emerged, without pulling it right through. Wind the thread round the needle point as many times as required. Holding the left thumb on the coiled thread, pull the needle through. Still holding the coiled thread, turn the needle back to where it was inserted and insert in the same place. Pull the needle through.

Herringbone stitches

Herringbone stitch

Closed herringbone stitch

Shadow work border

Double back stitch

Right angles in closed herringbone stitch

Shadow work with fringing

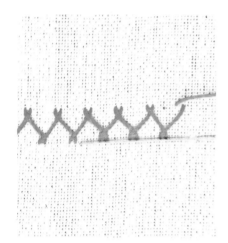

Herringbone stitch (*left*) Bring the needle out on the lower line at the left-hand side and insert on the upper line to the right, taking a stitch to the left with thread below needle. Next, insert the needle on the lower line to the right and take a stitch to the left with thread above needle.

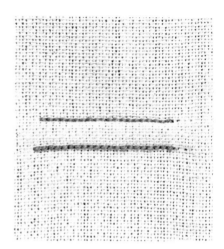

Double back stitch (*right*) This stitch is used in shadow work, and may also be called shadow stitch. Work from right to left. Insert the needle on the lower line and make a small back stitch. Bring needle out on upper line several threads to the left and make another back stitch. Bring needle out on lower line again, several threads to the left. Continue in this way.

Closed herringbone stitch (*left*) This is the reverse side of double back stitch. Work on the back of the fabric as for herringbone stitch, but leaving no space between the stitches. If a more obvious result is required for the shadow work, work the herringbone stitch over several threads laid the length of the row.

Right angles in closed herringbone stitch (*right*) Work a horizontal row of closed herringbone stitch as usual. To turn the corner, at the right angle, reduce the size of the inner stitches, but not the outer ones. When the right angle is completed, continue to work normally.

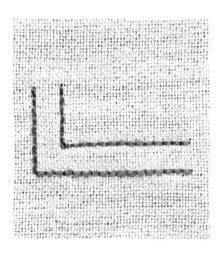

Fringed shadow work Shadow work may be used to form a border around a tablecloth or mat. To finish the edge attractively, fringing can be used. First work the border and corners in double back stitch (*left*). Trim the fabric leaving enough extra all round for the fringe. Next, pull the horizontal threads from around the edge. The vertical threads form the fringe (*right*).

Herringbone stitches
Double herringbone stitch
Interlaced herringbone stitch
Closed herringbone as filling stitch

Double herringbone stitch Working from left to right, make a row of simple herringbone stitch. Then, with a different colour, work a second row over the first so that the stitches alternate, using the free spaces.

Interlaced herringbone stitch Working from left to right, make a row of simple herringbone stitch. Then, with a contrasting colour, thread under the crossed stitch on the top line, and then on the bottom line, keeping the thread below the point of the needle. This stitch can be used in straight rows or to decorate a border.

Closed herringbone as a filling stitch 1 This is used to fill shapes with a curved outline, such as flower petals, leaves etc. In order to cover the area of the shape well, the stitches must be worked very closely, so that each new stitch touches the previous one.

Closed herringbone as a filling stitch 2 Fill in the area of the shape with closed herringbone stitch, as before. Then for greater impact, outline it in stem stitch, either in the same or in a contrasting colour.

Pekinese and Cretan stitches

Pekinese stitch   Interlaced Pekinese stitch
Cretan stitch   Open Cretan stitch

Pekinese stitch This is worked in two stages. First, make a row of fairly large back stitches. Then, working from left to right, loop a second thread through the bottom of the second stitch, back through the top of the first, up through the third and back down through the second, and so on. Pull the loops slightly to tighten them. Two colours or two thicknesses of thread can be used.

Interlaced Pekinese stitch Work two rows of fairly long back stitches. Working from right to left, pass the needle under the first stitch in the bottom row, and up through the second stitch in the top row. Pass the needle back down through the first stitch on the top row and under the third stitch on the bottom row. Pass up through the second stitch on the bottom row and up through the third stitch on the top row, then back down and under the second stitch on the top row, and so on.

Cretan stitch This is useful for filling small shapes. Work from left to right. Bring the thread through at the bottom left of the shape and take the needle back through at the top of the shape, making a small stitch towards the centre with the needle pointing inwards and the thread under the needle. Then take the needle through at the bottom of the shape, making another small stitch towards the centre with the needle pointing inwards and the thread under the needle as shown above. Continue in this way until the shape is filled.

Open Cretan stitch This is a useful border stitch. It is worked in the same way as Cretan stitch but, whereas this stitch follows the outlines of a shape, Open Cretan stitches are all the same height and are spaced at regular intervals.

Straight stitches
Free straight stitching
Tied straight stitching
Interlaced back stitch

Free straight stitching This is frequently used in floral designs to create the effect of foliage, and can be used in conjunction with the other stitches, such as stem stitch. It can be worked regularly or randomly, and the stitches can vary in length.

Tied straight stitching This can be used to fill leaf and petal shapes. Make a long stitch from left to right, bringing the needle out in the centre of the shape, one or two threads lower down. Then make a short couching stitch over the long one to hold it down, as shown. Bring the needle out at the left of the shape again, slightly higher up, and make another long stitch to the right. Hold this down with a short couching stitch and so on.

Interlaced back stitch Work two parallel lines of back stitch. With another thread of a contrasting colour, pass the needle up and under, then down and under the stitches of alternate back stitch rows.

Motifs using interlaced back stitch This stitch can be used to fill in areas of embroidered motifs such as the wings and body of these decorative beetles. The lines of back stitch need not be parallel – they can curve, as here.

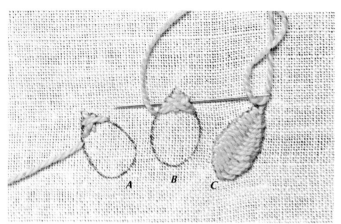

Fishbone stitch Bring the thread through at the top left of the shape. Make a sloping stitch across the central line. Bring the thread through opposite the first stitch, on the right of the shape, and make a similar sloping stitch to overlap the first stitch. Continue working alternately on each side until the shape is filled.

Raised fishbone stitch Bring the thread through just down from the top centre of the shape. Stitch into the top point. Come out down to the left and go in on the right, very close to the top. Come out again on the left and stitch down to the right to form two crossed stitches. Come out again on the left (***A***). Stitch up to the right (***B***), and come out to the left. Continue until the shape is filled (***C***).

Satin stitch 1. Working from left to right, bring the thread through on the lower edge of the shape and stitch into the opposite edge. Come out to the right of the first stitch, at a distance equal to the thickness of the thread being used, and stitch into the top edge in the same way.

2. Cover the entire surface of the shape. To achieve the smooth satin effect characteristic of this stitch, take care that the stitches are very even. To cover a large area, use an embroidery frame or ring, to ensure an even tension.

Padded stitches
Padded satin stitch   Circular padding
Double padding   Crossed padding

Padded satin stitch This is often used when working flowers and leaves. The relief effect is created by first working a thick, regular running stitch round the outline of a shape and then filling the centre with closely scattered stitches. Having worked this padding, cover it with satin stitch.

Circular padding When working circles with this method, the finished shape needs to be perfect, so it is necessary to use an embroidery frame. Outline the shape in running stitch and then fill the centre, staggering the stitches in each row. Finally, cover the shape with satin stitch, following the outline.

Double padding Use an embroidery frame when working circular shapes. Outline the shape with running stitch and then fill the centre with vertical rows of satin stitch. Next, cover the padding with satin stitch worked horizontally, following the outline precisely.

Crossed padding This is used when the circles to be covered are small. Outline the shape in running stitch, then pad the centre by using straight stitches worked one over the other to form a cross. Cover the shape with satin stitch, carefully following the outline.

Shading stitches

Long and short satin stitch   Split satin stitch
Block shading   Outline satin stitch

Long and short satin stitch As with all filling stitches, it is best to use a frame. Bring the needle through on the upper edge of the motif and, following the outline, make a row of alternately long and short stitches in towards the centre. Work the second row with stitches of equal length, fitting them into the stitches of the previous row. Continue working in this way until the motif is covered, combining various shades of colour to give a pleasing natural effect.

Split satin stitch Bring the thread through a short distance from the top of the motif and stitch back into the top. Bring the needle out a little way below this stitch and take it back through the centre of the first stitch, thus splitting it. Continue in this way. At the opposite edge of the motif, turn the work and proceed in the other direction.

Block shading When marking the design on the fabric, divide it into concentric or parallel sections. The sections are worked one after the other, either covering the surface of the design or leaving unstitched spaces between them. Start work in the outer section of the design, stitching inwards. Work towards the centre of the design on the following sections, interlocking the stitches very slightly with those of the previous row.

Outline satin stitch Work around the outline of the design, stitching inwards with a series of straight stitches of varying lengths to give a delicate effect. Use a thread with a sheen and soft colours for the best results.

Roumanian couching Work from left to right. Bring the thread through at the bottom of the motif and stitch into the top, coming out on the right three or four threads below. Make a small oblique tying stitch over the laid thread, coming out four or five threads down. Continue like this, covering the laid thread with little stitches.

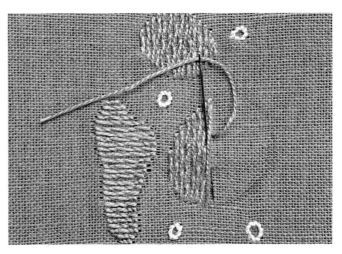

Brocade stitch This is a variation of the previous stitch. The method is the same; the laid thread is covered with small oblique tying stitches, but a small space is left between the laid threads so that each stitch is separate from the next. The finished effect is of old, worn brocade.

Roumanian stitch Bring the thread through at the top edge of the motif. Stitch to the opposite edge and come out on the centre line to the right of the first stitch. Make a small tying stitch, bringing the needle out again at the top edge of the motif. Continue in this way.

Double buttonhole stitch This can be used as a covering stitch on small designs, such as leaves and petals. Work two rows of interlocking buttonhole stitch, one along the lower edge, and the second along the opposite edge, fitting into the spaces left by the first row. On the second row it is easier to turn the work so that the working edge is always the lower one.

Cross stitches

Cross stitch worked in two stages The first stage is worked from left to right and the second from right to left. Bring the thread through to the right side of the fabric, and make a diagonal stitch up to the right over the required number of threads. Stitch down over an equal number of threads and continue in this way until the row is completed. On the return row, repeat the process in reverse, completing the crosses.

Spaced cross stitch Work in two stages, spacing the crosses as required. Having decided how far apart the stitches should be, work a row of diagonal stitches of equal size from left to right. Complete the crosses on the return row from right to left, making sure that the stitches are the same size.

Cross stitch worked from the left Bring the thread through to the right side of the fabric. Stitch diagonally down to the left, coming out vertically, level with the top of the stitch. Stitch diagonally to the right into the lower stitching line, completing the cross. Next, stitch diagonally to the right to start the second cross.

Cross stitch worked from the right Bring the thread through to the right side of the fabric, and stitch diagonally up to the right. Come out vertically downwards and complete the cross by stitching diagonally up to the left. Come out diagonally down to the left and start the second stitch.

Two-sided insertion stitch Stitch diagonally up over nine threads and three to the right. Come out down to the right with a diagonal stitch on the reverse of the fabric, three threads in height and width. Stitch horizontally to the left over six threads. Come out at the top of the first long stitch. Go in again six threads to the right of the base of the first stitch and come out up to the left with a diagonal on the reverse of the fabric, three threads in height and width as shown above. Make a diagonal up to the left over three threads, coming out at the beginning of the same stitch. Make another diagonal to the right, again over three threads, coming out at the beginning of the same stitch. Then make a horizontal stitch over six threads to the right. Come out at the base of the second long diagonal. Starting from this point, make the next long diagonal to the right.

One-sided insertion stitch Make a diagonal stitch up to the right over three threads in height and width. Come out horizontally three threads to the left and stitch diagonally down to complete the simple cross. Come out horizontally three threads to the left, then make a long diagonal up to the right, three threads wide and six high. Come out horizontally three threads to the left. Complete the irregular cross down to the right, going in at the top of the first stitch. Come out six threads horizontally to the left. Make the second simple cross, coming out at the top left to make the long arm of the irregular cross, six threads down and three to the right. Come out horizontally left and stitch diagonally up to the right to complete the irregular cross. Come out six threads to the left to make the third simple cross and so on.

Montenegrin cross stitch Work in rows from left to right. Bring the needle through to the right side of the fabric and make a diagonal stitch to the right over eight vertical and four horizontal threads. Come out four threads to the right of the base of the first stitch and make a diagonal stitch up to the left over four threads. Come out at the beginning of the same stitch. Stitch vertically upwards over four threads, again coming out at the same point as before. Start the next stitch by making a second long diagonal to the right.

Long-armed cross stitch Work in rows from left to right. Bring the needle through to the right side of the fabric and stitch up to the right over eight vertical and four horizontal threads. Come out four threads vertically downwards. Stitch diagonally up to the left over four threads in height and width and come out four threads vertically downwards. Begin the second stitch by making another long diagonal.

Holbein or Double running stitch
Holbein stitch border
Holbein stitch motifs
Holbein stitch variations

Holbein or Double running stitch border This is made up of a double line of running stitch worked in two stages. The finished effect is like back stitch. Work the first row from left to right. Following the pattern on a chart, make a line of equally spaced running stitches (the stitches must be the same length as the space between them). For the second row, work in the same way from right to left, filling in the spaces left in the first row until the starting point is reached.

Holbein or Double running stitch motifs This shows two completed motifs worked in Holbein stitch on evenweave fabric. Although they are made up of straight stitches, the flower petals look as though they have a curved outline. Use an embroidery frame for Holbein stitch and pull the thread up gently when working so as not to distort the fabric. Holbein stitch is used in the technique called Assisi work described on the opposite page.

Holbein stitch variation 1 This can be worked in straight or curved lines. Working from right to left, bring the thread through to the right side of the work and, holding the needle pointing horizontally left, make a vertical stitch upwards. Come out three fabric threads away to the left. Now make a vertical stitch downwards, again coming out three threads away to the left. Continue to the end of the row. Work the second row from left to right, passing the needle under the bars without picking up the fabric threads. Come out at the centre right of the first bar and pass the needle under the bar from right to left and upwards. Then pass the needle under the second bar from right to left and downwards. Repeat to the end of the row.

Holbein stitch variation 2 This looks similar to four-sided stitch, but is worked in two diagonal stages, top to bottom, then bottom to top. Being double-sided, it is also useful on fine or transparent fabrics. In stage **A**, work a series of vertical stitches diagonally downwards to the left as shown, bringing the needle out horizontally each time to begin the next stitch. At the end of the row, begin the second stage, **B**. This time work a series of horizontal stitches diagonally upwards, bringing the needle out vertically each time to begin the next stitch. This completes the row of squares.

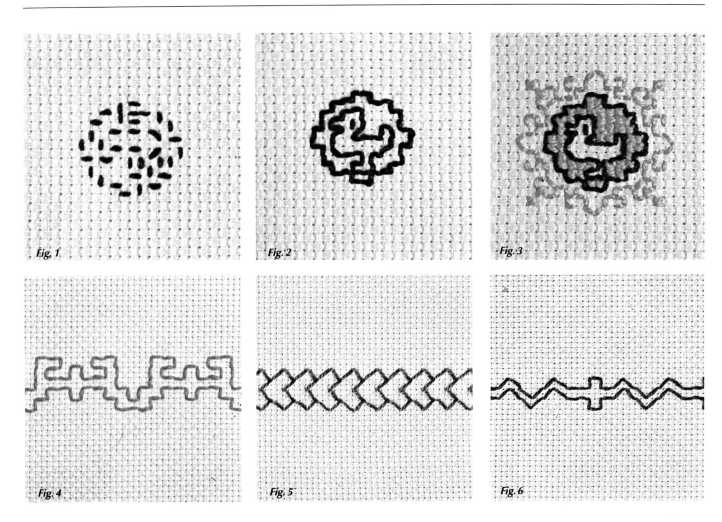

Fig. 1

Fig. 2

Fig. 3

Fig. 4

Fig. 5

Fig. 6

This distinctive form of embroidery takes its name from the town of Assisi in Italy where it has its origins. The stylized animals, birds and other motifs characteristic of this type of work are inspired by ancient embroideries which are still carefully preserved in the churches of the area, and also by designs found in other works of art such as mosaics, marble sculptures, wood carvings and inlay work. The method of embroidery used to produce these bold designs set inside geometric borders has remained unchanged over the centuries.

Materials The fabric used for this form of embroidery must have an even weave.

The thread used to work the filling around the shapes is traditionally blue or rust, and that for the outline is black.

Method The work is done in three stages; the outline, the filling and the finishing off. Following the design on a chart, work the first row of Holbein stitch (**Fig. 1**) as described on the opposite page.
Return along the row of stitching filling in the gaps, passing under the previous stitches and making sure that the outline of the design is continuous. The outline is worked in black to contrast with the filling (**Fig. 2**).
Having finished the outline, start the filling in cross stitch worked in two stages, first in one direction and then in the other (**Fig. 3**).

Make sure that the stitching on the reverse of the fabric is as perfect as that on the right side.
Figs. 4, 5 and 6 show examples of linear patterns used in Assisi work.
Finishing off the work with a decorative hem is important. The hem should be as narrow as possible, giving a corded effect. It is made by rolling the fabric between the thumb and forefinger of the left hand while work is in progress. The hems are often decorated with regular slanting oversewing stitches and the corners of the finished cloth are sometimes decorated with little tassels.

Threaded satin stitch This stitch is worked in two stages: the first makes the vertical satin stitch blocks and the second the zigzag lines. To begin with, work a row of satin stitch blocks, each made up of three bars worked over six threads of fabric. Leave four threads of fabric between each block. On the return row, work the blocks so they alternate with those in the first row. Continue until the surface of the work is covered in this way. Move on to the second stage. Bring the needle through on the right hand side of the work and pass it horizontally under the first satin stitch block from right to left without picking up the fabric. Then pass the needle under the next block in the row above, then under the next block in the first row and so on.

Zigzag filling stitch Work in two rows, one going from left to right and the other returning from right to left. Bring the needle through to the right side of the fabric and make a diagonal stitch five threads down and five to the left. Come out five threads to the right of the top of the first stitch. Stitch down again, five threads to the right of the base of the first stitch. Continue like this, making a row of small diagonal stitches. Work the following row below the first. Make the second part of the zigzag, stitching up and to the left, going in at the base of the stitches in the previous row.

Basket filling stitch This is worked in two stages, each going from left to right. Bring the needle through to the right side of the fabric and stitch vertically up over six threads. Work another three stitches in this way on successive threads to make a block of four stitches. Move five threads to the right and work another block of stitches. Complete the row in this way. Turn the work and start the second stage, again moving from left to right. Work blocks of satin stitch as before, fitting them into the spaces left by the previous row and overlapping by three fabric threads. Work the third row the same as the first.

Squared filling stitch This stitch creates the effect of squares on the diagonal and is worked in rows from left to right and vice versa. Bring the needle through to the right side of the fabric and stitch diagonally up to the right, four threads up and four along. Come out on the lower line eight threads to the right. Now make a stitch up to the left, going in at the top of the preceding stitch. Bring the needle out at the base of the stitch just worked. Repeat the stitch to the right and then to the left to form a zigzag line. Work the return row below, so the zigzag points coincide to form the squares. The third row is started eight threads below, with another zigzag line.

Reversing 'V' stitch Work each row in two stages. For the first row, begin working from left to right. Stitch diagonally down over two threads and over four to the right. Work a second stitch in the same way, beginning eight threads to the right, and so on to the end of the row. The return row from right to left completes the 'V' with the diagonal stitches sloping the other way. The third row is worked in the same way as the second from right to left, staggering the stitches as shown.

Eye stitch Work in horizontal rows. Bring the needle through to the right side of the fabric, stitch vertically up over three threads and come out again at the base of the same stitch. Stitch up to the left, over a diagonal of three threads and come out again at the same point; in the same way stitch horizontally to the left over three threads, diagonally down to the left, vertically down, diagonally down to the right, horizontally to the right, and diagonally up to the right, always over three threads. Having made the first eye, start a second, twelve threads to the right. On the return row, alternate the eyes with those in the first.

Triangle filling stitch Work in rows, from left to right and right to left. Bring the thread through to the right side of the fabric and make a vertical stitch up over two threads. Come out on the base line one thread to the right and stitch up again, this time over four threads and then over six and eight threads. Complete the triangle by stitching over six, four and two threads. Then work the next triangle as before. Work the return row from right to left in the same way.

Star squares Begin at top left of the motif. Bring the needle through to the right side of the fabric and stitch down over three threads, then diagonally left over three threads, and horizontally left over three threads, always stitching back into the same point. Come out three vertical threads down and stitch back into the same point. Come out diagonally down, three threads to the left to begin the second star. Stitch horizontally, diagonally, vertically and then horizontally again to make the second star, always working over three threads. Make the third and fourth stars in the same way. This completes one motif.

Block and diamond filling stitch First make a network of small, parallel, diagonal stitches over two threads of the fabric. These form small diamonds where the lines intersect. Inside the resulting spaces work satin stitch rectangles eight threads high and nine stitches wide.

Trellis filling stitch This background is very simple, and gives an effective result. One colour only is used. Work horizontal rows, angling one stitch to the right and then one to the left, over two threads in height and four in width. In the following row alternate the slope of the stitches.

Star network First work the groups of stars, each group having four stars. Each star is made of two diagonal stitches, a horizontal stitch and a vertical stitch, one on top of the other. Link the groups of stars with short horizontal and longer vertical stitches.

Basketweave filling stitch The first stage is to work the chequered effect of the background. Each section is made up of blocks of four satin stitches worked horizontally over five threads, alternating on each row. The second stage completes the pattern with pairs of vertical stitches worked in the spaces left between the satin stitch blocks.

Block and cross filling stitch Work the tied satin stitch blocks first. These consist of four vertical stitches worked over six fabric threads. Having worked the last stitch, come out at the centre left of the first stitch and work a horizontal stitch to the right. Work a second block seven threads to the right and so on. Alternate the position of the blocks in each row. Then fill the spaces with crossed diagonal stitches over the same number of threads as the satin stitch blocks.

Diagonal block filling stitch First work the diagonal stitches, three at a time, over four threads of the fabric. The blocks of stitches slope first to the right and then to the left. Leave two threads between each block. In the next row, the slope of the stitches alternates. The spaces left are filled with cross stitches over four threads of fabric.

Double cross filling stitch First work cross stitch over six threads of the fabric, stitching diagonally from left to right and then from right to left. Next work a second cross with one vertical and one horizontal stitch, making a small cross over the first. Make a second large cross stitch six threads to the right of the first. On the second row alternate the crosses in the spaces left. To finish the pattern, work diagonal stitches over four threads at the point where the long diagonals meet.

Grains of rice filling stitch Bring the needle through to the right side of the fabric and work a horizontal stitch from left to right over six threads of the fabric. Repeat the stitch one thread lower. Then bring the needle up at the centre of the first stitch and take down at the centre of the second stitch, forming a small vertical tying stitch. Work the second group of stitches six threads to the right. The second row is worked one thread lower and the groups of stitches alternate with the spaces left in the first row.

Drawn thread work
Preparing the fabric
Cable stitch
Rhodes or Single faggot stitch

Preparing the fabric To draw a thread from either the warp or weft of the fabric, just lift the thread with the point of a needle and snip carefully with sharp scissors. Then gently pull it out. If several threads are to be drawn out, snip them in the middle of the row, draw out towards the edges and darn them in to prevent fraying. Care needs to be taken when the drawn thread turns a corner. First mark the diagonal with a crease. Work out the position of the corner and mark with a pin (**A**). At this point cut both the weft and warp threads and carefully pull them out as far as the next corner to be made (**B**).

Cable stitch 1. Make a drawn thread row, withdrawing two or three threads, depending on the thickness of the fabric and the thread. Bring the needle through to the right side, in the row of drawn threads. Holding the needle pointing horizontally to the left, make a stitch to the right over an even number of threads. Come out halfway along to the left, holding the thread below the needle.

2. Make a second horizontal stitch to the right, over the same number of threads as the first stitch, coming out halfway along to the left but this time holding the thread above the needle. Continue in this way, pulling the thread slightly.

Rhodes stitch or Single faggot stitch This is a drawn fabric stitch, worked without withdrawing any threads, and can be used to decorate table linen with drawn thread borders. Pull the stitches firmly while working. It is worked on the diagonal. Bring the needle through to the right side of the fabric, and stitch horizontally to the right, joining the base of the previous vertical stitch and coming out diagonally down to the left (**A**). Make a vertical stitch upwards, this time joining the previous horizontal stitch (**B**) and coming out diagonally to the left. Continue in this way.

Drawn thread work

Italian squared ground | Italian squared ground (reverse)
Sewing a hem with Italian squared ground | Hemstitch worked in interlocking rows

Italian squared ground Work on a double row of pulled threads, calculated so as to be able to divide the row into squares. Work from right to left, bringing the thread through to the right side of the fabric in the lower row. Make a horizontal stitch to the right over three (or the chosen number of) threads. Come out diagonally left in the upper row, as show above, forming a diagonal stitch on the reverse of the work. Stitch horizontally to the right, coming out at the beginning of the same stitch. Make a vertical stitch downwards, then come out three threads to the left to begin another square.

Italian squared ground (reverse) Work from left to right on the wrong side of the fabric. Bring the thread through on the lower line of pulled threads and work a horizontal stitch over the chosen number of threads. Come out again at the beginning of the stitch. Stitch diagonally up to the right into the upper row of pulled threads, coming out horizontally to the left, as shown above. Make a stitch to the right to meet the diagonal stitch and come out vertically down. Continue as before. A row of squares is formed on the other side of the fabric.

Sewing a hem with Italian squared ground Pull the first row of threads, then fold and tack the hem so that the fold lies along the row of drawn threads. Make a second row of pulled threads at the desired distance. Work on the reverse of the fabric. Bring the thread through from the inside of the folded hem to the right side of the fold. Make a diagonal stitch to the right into the drawn thread row and come out vertically up into the opposite row of drawn threads. Then make a horizontal stitch to the right, coming out again at the beginning of the stitch. Take the thread diagonally down to the lower drawn thread row, coming out horizontally to the left and reinserting the needle through the folded hem as shown.

Hemstitch worked in interlocking rows Work a fishbone pattern vertically from top to bottom in two stages, having made a double row of drawn threads. Work the first stage on the left. Pass the needle down behind several threads along the drawn thread line, come out, then insert the needle behind the same threads, coming out at the centre of the two rows of drawn threads with a diagonal stitch. Stitch back into the bottom of the vertical stitch and continue in this way. Work the second row of stitches to interlock with the first.

Hemstitch This is worked along a border of threads pulled from either the weft or the warp of the fabric. Bring the needle through one or two threads below the drawn thread border. Working from left to right, make a small diagonal stitch to the right, passing the needle horizontally to the left behind a number of the loose threads. Pull the needle through carefully, gathering the threads together. Stitch back behind the fabric, coming out below the drawn threads, as shown above. Stitch again to the right, gathering the same number of loose threads and so on.

Ladder hemstitch First work a row of hemstitch at the base of a border of drawn threads. Turn the work round and work a second row along the opposite edge, picking up the same threads gathered into groups in the first row. The stitch can also be worked along the top edge without turning the work, as shown. Bring the needle through to the right side of the work to the left of the first group of threads, collect this group of threads by stitching horizontally to the left, pulling the thread through carefully. Then make a small diagonal stitch up and to the right. Bring the needle out in the drawn threads again with a small vertical stitch.

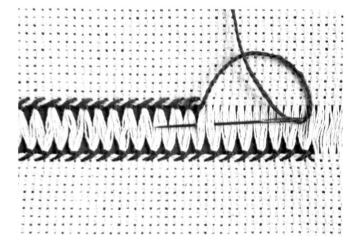

Zigzag hemstitch This is another double hemstitch, worked on both sides of a border of drawn threads. On either side of the border make a row of simple hemstitch, working from left to right. Gather up an even number of threads. On working the second row the stitches are made into the centre of each of the groups of threads gathered in the first row. As in ladder hemstitch the second row can be made without turning the work, as shown.

Drawn thread work
Double knotted zigzag border
Wide double knotted border
Buttonhole stitch border

Double knotted zigzag border With this stitch it is not neces-sary to finish the edges of the drawn thread band, but this should not be too wide. Secure the sewing thread at the right-hand side. Make the first knot with the sewing thread looped into a coral knot stitch as shown, catching four threads together. Move up to the left, catching together two threads from the first group and two free ones. Continue in this way, always knotting together two threads from the previous group and two free ones, working up and down in a zigzag.

Wide double knotted border This needs a wide, hemstitched section of drawn threads, on which a double knotted effect is worked. Secure the sewing thread at the right-hand side. Always working over one third of the height, knot four groups of threads together. Take the sewing thread behind two of the threads, and moving down, knot together these two and two more, as shown. Continue in this way, zigzagging up and down.

Buttonhole stitch border Work on a wide hemstitched section of drawn threads. The work requires accuracy. Secure the sewing thread at the right-hand side and start at the centre of the drawn threads, working buttonhole stitch over three threads and finish-ing at about a quarter of their height. At this point make a stitch that takes in three new threads, and then continue working only on the new threads. Continue working zigzag fashion to the end of the first row. Work the return row over the incomplete section of work opposite the zigzag, completing the diamond shape in a symmetrical manner.

Drawn thread work

Vertical bars   Zigzag bars
Double woven bars   Five column woven bars

Vertical bars Bring the needle through to the right side of the work and take the thread across to the opposite side of the drawn thread border. This thread serves as a guide and is covered, along with a group of the vertical threads, by simply winding the sewing thread round them in an overcasting stitch. Having finished the bar, stitch through the back of the work and come out again ready to start the next one. The bars are worked from right to left.

Zigzag bars This uses the same method as the previous example, without the need for the guide thread. Overcast three drawn threads to the opposite edge of the drawn thread border. Then make a longer stitch over another three threads to the right as shown, and proceed to cover these three only. Continue in this way. The zigzag results from the longer stitch, which joins two groups of threads together each time.

Double woven bars The illustration above shows how the sewing thread is woven in and out of the fabric threads. Work from left to right. To begin, lay the thread end along the first four fabric threads. Pass the needle over the first two fabric threads and under the second two. Then pass the needle back over the second two threads and under the first two, grouping the four threads and the thread end together in a figure-of-eight movement. Continue in this way until the bar is covered, and finish off by threading through the back of the worked bar.

Five column woven bars The method is identical to the previous example, weaving in and out of five threads instead of two. This method can also be used on larger numbers of threads, but in this case greater precision is required. The number of vertical threads in the drawn thread border should be worked out in multiples of the number of threads used for each bar.

158

Drawn thread work
Preparing drawn corners
Corners with web filling

Preparing drawn corners 1. An empty square is left at the corners when the threads for a border have been withdrawn. These three stages illustrate how to work a perfect corner. Decide on the position of the corner and make two cuts at the inner right angle. Pull the weft and warp threads for the borders away from this angle.

2. Successively draw the threads of the square determined by the two border rows. Fold the freed threads to the reverse of the work and stitch them in place with a thread the same colour as the fabric. In the illustration the thread is of a contrasting colour for greater clarity.

3. Work the edges of the square in buttonhole or satin stitch, so that they are completely covered and will not fray. Trim any excess threads from the edges on the reverse of the fabric, taking care not to damage the stitching.

Corners with web filling If the borders of drawn threads are fairly wide, the resulting corner will be correspondingly large and will need the support of diagonal, horizontal and vertical stitches, decorated in various ways, to help it keep its shape. In this example the centre is covered with a web, made by passing the needle alternately over and under the threads.

Hardanger embroidery takes its name from a district of Western Norway. It is based on stitches used in drawn thread and counted thread work and can have a very elaborate appearance. The fabric used should have a precise even weave and the thread should be chosen to suit the fabric. The basic blocks are worked in satin stitch which is used in conjunction with woven bars and various filling stitches.

Satin stitch This can be worked in a continuous manner to form bands of embroidery (*1A*). Alternatively it can be worked in blocks (*1B*) which form decorative patterns and can be arranged in a square formation with drawn threads at the centre. It is best to use an embroidery frame for this.

Diagonal satin stitch Diagonal patterns are often used. With each stitch, move one thread up and sideways (*2A*) following the line of work. Satin stitch blocks can also be staggered, by stitching first vertically and then horizontally over a chosen number of threads, the corners meeting (*2B*).

Satin stitch blocks in square formation This border consists of a series of satin stitch blocks arranged in a square formation. While working each section, make sure that the fabric is kept taut. Complete the work by cutting away the centre threads (*3A*) or by making the hole with the help of a bodkin (*3B*) in which case the threads are not cut but are oversewn with tight stitches.

Woven bars Work satin stitch blocks in a square formation, each side consisting of two blocks. When this is done, cut the threads as shown in *4A*. Then make woven bars (*4B*), weaving the threads two at a time as explained on page 158.

Hardanger embroidery
Diamond shapes   Web stitch
Weaving stitch   Triangular shapes

Diamond shapes First work the outline of the shape in satin stitch blocks over four threads of the fabric. The blocks are made of either three or five satin stitches. Withdraw the threads leaving a central rectangle (**A**). Outline the edges of the rectangle with an overcasting stitch and work loop stitch at the centre (**B**).

Web stitch Make a long diagonal stitch upwards and work back down over it, forming a row with a similar appearance to cross stitch (**A**). Work further rows to intermesh (**B**). The spacing of the diagonal lines and the length of the stitches can vary according to the effect required.

Weaving stitch 1. Work the base stitching, taking care to cross the threads as shown above (**A**). Having done this, return to the right side of the work with a small stitch, picking up a single thread of fabric (**B**).

2. Start to weave through the base threads without picking up any of the underlying fabric. The needle is passed under and over the base stitching in the order shown, starting at the bottom left-hand corner (**C**). Work right round clockwise (**D**).

3. When the weaving is complete, finish off the thread at the back of the work.

Triangular shapes The outline is worked in satin stitch blocks consisting of three stitches worked either horizontally or vertically over four threads of the fabric. Withdraw threads from the inner area and decorate these remaining with overcasting and woven bars.

161

Broderie anglaise 1. This form of work falls into the category of cut work and is based on a design of round and oval eyelets. These are made either by piercing the fabric with a bodkin or, with larger eyelets, by cutting and turning back the fabric. The embroidery is worked entirely in white. Before starting the work, mark out the design on the fabric using dressmaker's carbon paper and a well sharpened pencil.

2. To keep the work as precise as possible, the fabric may be attached to a paper backing with tacking stitches. This keeps the work firm. Work round the outlines of the patterns marked on the fabric with very small running stitches to strengthen them.

3. Cover the base stitches with very fine, close, regular oversewing stitches so that the outlines of the patterns show up well. Remove the backing paper.

4. Pierce the centre of the eyelets with a bodkin, pushing it first through from the right side and then through from the reverse of the fabric, so that the weave of the fabric is stretched well. If the holes in the pattern are larger, it is advisable to cut and turn back the fabric before the final stitching.

Pisa work This differs from broderie anglaise in that the cut areas are rather larger and need bars across them to hold the edges together. A firmly woven fabric is required, which is tacked onto stiff paper while working the embroidery to prevent it stretching out of shape. Mark the design onto the fabric with dressmaker's carbon paper. Work a row of small running stitches around the edge of the design and at the first bar, cross it with a long stitch to the opposite side and then back again to continue with the running stitch. Do this each time a bar is reached (**A**). Complete the running stitch around the edge (**B**). Then returning over the same stitches, complete the bars without picking up any of the fabric beneath by working oversewing around them (**C**). Cut the fabric at the centre of the design and fold it back around the edges (**D**). Oversew around the edges to secure them (**E**).

Richelieu embroidery Another way of covering the edges and bars of the design is with buttonhole stitch. Here, once the running stitch outline and bars have been worked, they are covered with buttonhole stitch. Begin the buttonhole stitch around the edge of the design. Then, on reaching a bar, take a third long stitch across to the opposite side and work back over the bar only with buttonhole stitch. Continue around the edge to the next bar. When the embroidery is complete, remove the backing paper and very carefully cut away the fabric right up to the edge of the buttonhole stitch.

Fig. 1

Fig. 2

Fig. 3

Fig. 4

Smocking was originally used to decorate the loose overgarments worn by farm workers in rural England. It spread from England and was soon in general use in many countries. The stitches used in smocking include stem stitch, chain stitch, cross stitch and any stitches that are slightly elastic.

Preparing the fabric The work is carried out in two stages: first the preparation, when the fabric is gathered into pleats, and secondly, working the decorative embroidery stitches over the gathers. Once the gathers are regular, stroke them into even parallel lines with the head of a large needle. It is helpful to use a fabric with regular points of reference such as checks, small repeating designs or stripes (*Fig. 1*). With plain fabric, which has no points of reference, smocking dots must be marked first. Iron-on transfers with rows of smocking dots are available. Alternatively the fabric can be marked in other ways. The first method requires a sheet of squared paper and a pencil sharp enough to pierce the paper. Place the paper in position on the reverse side of the fabric and pierce it, forming a small dot on the fabric where the vertical and horizontal lines of the squared paper cross

(*Fig. 2*). Continue across the fabric, moving the paper along carefully if necessary, until the row is completed. The second method is to use a ruler and the point of a large needle. With the ruler as a guide, prick the fabric in a series of parallel equally-spaced lines which will indicate where to gather the fabric. If the fabric has vertical stripes, just the horizontal lines need to be pricked, but if the fabric is plain, prick both horizontal and vertical lines, using the intersections as the dots. Using a long thread with a large knot in the end, start gathering from right to left. With the point of the needle, pick up several threads of the fabric at each dot (*Fig. 3*). At the end of each row, unthread the needle and leave the thread hanging. When all the rows are completed, pull the hanging threads, two at a time, to the required width, then fasten the threads with a firm knot. For the best results, the width of the fabric to be gathered should be three times the required finished width.

Outline stitch This basic stitch (*Fig. 4*) is similar to stem stitch and is usually worked from left to right. Each pleat, or group of pleats, corresponds to one stitch. The thread must be held either always above or always below the needle.

Cable stitch Cable stitch is a firm control stitch. Hold the needle horizontally, with the thread alternately above and below the needle, working through two pleats at a time.

Wave stitch Make a row of ascending horizontal stitches, and using the top stitch as a joining stitch, make a descending row of stitches, changing the position of the thread. On the ascending row the thread is below the needle, and on the descending row it is above. This stitch can be made less elastic by using one new pleat and one previous one (as in the top row), instead of two new ones (as in the bottom row).

Herringbone stitch This smocking stitch is similar to ordinary herringbone stitch. Working from left to right, sew through the first pleat on the left. The first stitch is made diagonally up and to the right, picking up the pleats horizontally from right to left. The next stitch is made diagonally down and to the right, again picking up the pleats from right to left. Each stitch picks up two or more pleats and the thread is pulled through gently. Continue working to the right, making one stitch on the top sewing line, and one on the bottom.

Chain stitch The elasticity of this stitch depends on the firmness of the smocking. If maximum elasticity is required, work in zigzags. Moving from right to left, sew through the first pleat on the right and work the first chain, picking up the first and second pleats. Work the second chain by picking up the second and third pleats, and so on. Continue along the row in a zigzag fashion.

Feather stitch This stitch can be made in various ways, as with ordinary feather stitch. Hold the smocking so that the thread is always towards you and then work from right to left and vice-versa to form the zigzags. Start at the first pleat on the right. To make the first stitch, pick up the first and second pleats catching the thread under the point of the needle. Work the second stitch, picking up the second and third pleats, and so on, according to the number of stitches planned. Turn the work and start the next row from left to right. Continue in a zigzag manner.

Double feather stitch Work two rows of double feather stitch in opposite directions. Turn the work for each row so that the work proceeds in the right direction. Double feather stitch is quite tight and can be used to firm the smocking, at the same time producing a pretty decorative effect.

Diamond stitch This stitch is completed in two rows. Work from left to right. Start at the first pleat on the left. Take the thread up and to the right and pick up the next pleat, passing the needle from right to left. Now make a horizontal stitch, passing the needle through the following pleat from right to left. Take the thread down and to the right, and pick up the following pleat from right to left. Make another horizontal stitch, passing the needle from right to left through the next pleat. Complete the first row in this way. Work the second row so that the horizontal stitches coincide and the characteristic shape of the stitch is formed.

Vandyke stitch This stitch is worked from right to left. Bring the needle through to the right side of the work at the second pleat from the right. Make a back stitch over the first two pleats. Take the needle down to the row below. Pick up the second and third pleats and make a back stitch over them. Take the needle back up to the row above. Pick up the third and fourth pleats and make a back stitch over them. Return to the row below and continue in this way to the end of the row. The next line of stitching is worked in the same manner, beginning on the third row down and taking the needle up to the second row where the back stitches will coincide.

Cross stitch A single row of cross stitch can be used to arrange the gathers in the smocking. Plan out the area of smocking on which you wish to work, and the height of the stitches. Working from right to left, take the needle through four pleats to the left, make a diagonal stitch up to the right and then stitch through the same four pleats to the left. Complete the cross by stitching to the bottom right and out at the starting point. Repeat this to form a continuous row of small, joined crosses. Working on a checked fabric, such as gingham, makes the work easier. This stitch gives only a slight elasticity.

Back stitch This is a simple stitch used to firm the gathers. The result is only slightly elastic. To make the stitch, pick up one pleat with the needle and stitch through three pleats to the left. Back stitch over one pleat and again stitch through three to the left. Continue in this way to the end of the row. The result will be a succession of free pleats and pleats held by the back stitch. Stagger the rows so that the back stitches hold the free pleats in alternate rows.

Surface honeycomb stitch 1 Work from left to right. Stitch through the first pleat on the left and make an upward slanting stitch round the pleat with the needle pointing from right to left. Make a second stitch in the same way. Then make a horizontal stitch to the right, picking up the second pleat to the right and coming out between the two pleats. Repeat the two slanting stitches downwards, make another horizontal stitch picking up the third pleat, then start the upward slanting stitches again. Continue in a zigzag manner. A second row beneath the first completes the diamond pattern.

Surface honeycomb stitch 2 This is an extended version of the previous stitch, the diagonals being longer and held firmly by two horizontal stitches at top and bottom in order to strengthen the stitch at these points. Complete the diamond pattern with a second row below.

Fig. 1

Appliqué is the technique of arranging pieces of fabric on a contrasting background and securing them with decorative embroidery stitches. The applied fabric can be in the form of leaves, flowers or other small decorative designs. The stitches used for securing the shapes can be divided into two main groups: those which border an unhemmed edge which is later trimmed and those which are worked over a small single hem to prevent fraying. The first group includes buttonhole stitch and oversewing and the second straight stitch, stem stitch, chain stitch and cross stitch.

Stitch and cut appliqué With this method, the shapes are applied with a border of fabric left around them. This is cut off when the embroidery is complete. Prepare the work by carefully marking out the design on the right side of the background fabric. Also mark the shapes on the appliqué fabric, leaving a margin of fabric all round. Place the appliqué pieces on the corresponding outlines on the background fabric and stitch the two fabrics together with a small running stitch around the edge of the shapes (**Fig. 1**). Baste the outer margin of the appliqué fabric to the background fabric away from the design outlines. Iron thoroughly, then work around the design with the chosen stitch. Trim the excess fabric as below.

Fig. 2

Fig. 3

Buttonhole stitch Secure the appliqué pieces with buttonhole stitch so that the base line of the stitching is at the outer edge of the shape (**Fig. 2**). Stitch firmly and continuously, following the line of the design. When the stitching is complete, remove the tacking and press with a warm iron on the reverse side. Finally cut away any excess fabric with a pair of very sharp scissors, taking care not to damage the stitching thread. If there are a lot of shapes to be applied, make sure that the threads of both the shapes and the background fabric run the same way.

Oversewing stitch Prepare the work and then edge the appliqué shape in close oversewing stitch (**Fig. 3**). Cut away the excess fabric, leaving only the narrowest of margins. This stitch is most commonly used to apply lightweight fabrics, such as fine linen or organza.

Fig. 4

Fig. 5

Reverse appliqué In this method, two layers of fabric are placed together, one on top of the other. Mark the outline of the motif on the top layer, then work small running stitches around it through both layers. Cut away the top layer of fabric from inside the motif (**Fig. 4**). Finish the edges with close oversewing stitch worked through both layers (**Fig. 5**). This method can be used as a border on a wide hem or on tablecloths and other household linen. It it not suitable for use over a wide surface area.

Preparing the hemmed appliqué 1. Mark out the design on both the background fabric and on the fabric to be applied. Cut out the appliqué shape, allowing an extra 5mm ($\frac{3}{16}$in) all round to turn under.

2. Tack this hem to the wrong side with small stitches, folding it under carefully so as not to spoil the shape. With a curved shape, tiny folds can be made at right angles to the edge to make the hemming easier and neater.

3. Now tack the hemmed shape to the background fabric to match the previously marked out design. To prevent the shape from moving, pin it at various places. Tack the shape into place with even stitches along the edge, finishing off with a couple of small firm stitches. Work the chosen embroidery stitch around the shape, then remove the tacking thread and press lightly on both sides.

Securing with slipstitch Having prepared and tacked the appliqué shape in place, sew it into position with small, even stitches. Work from right to left, picking up first a thread of the background fabric and then of the appliqué shape to make a line of neat, slanting stitches.

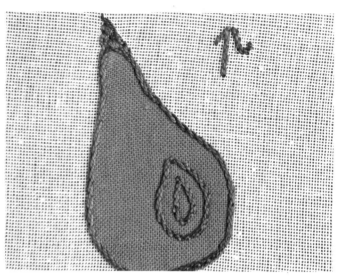

Straight stitch   This is used to create a textured, irregular edging. First make a border of stitches of the same length, then, in a second row, intersperse these with longer or overlapping stitches.

Stem stitch   Using short, close stitches, work around the folded edge of an appliqué shape. Further rows can be added around the edge at varying distances apart, either on the appliqué shape itself or on the background fabric.

Chain stitch   This stitch is particularly useful on curving shapes such as trees, clouds or petals. The first row is stitched all round the edge of the shape and then spirals towards the centre two or more times.

Cross stitch   This is best used on motifs with straight edges. To make sure that the appliqué shape is accurate, first rule a line on the appliqué fabric, then fold the hem under and tack the shape to the background fabric. With evenweave fabrics, the stitches can be worked as in counted thread work. Work the cross stitch in two stages, counting the threads to ensure that the stitches are of uniform size.

Applying lace
Making a lace-edged border
Paris stitch
Three-sided stitch

Making a lace-edged border This can be done in two ways. The first is for medium thickness fabric. Tack the lace 1cm (⅜in) from the edge of the fabric. Stitch it with the chosen embroidery stitch, then cut off the excess fabric. The second method is for finer fabrics. Place the lace 1cm (⅜in) from the edge of the fabric, tack it and oversew it with a fine thread. Remove the tacking and fold down the edge of the fabric. Finish off the lace with the chosen stitch, sewing through the folded edge. Lastly, cut away the surplus fabric.

Paris stitch This is an excellent stitch to use when applying fine fabric, as well as for lace as in this example. Work from right to left. Bring the needle through the fabric and make a small back stitch, bringing the needle out diagonally through the lace, above the beginning of the back stitch. Make a vertical stitch back down to this point, then bring the needle out through the fabric one stitch to the left. Continue as before. The thread used in the illustration for clarity should, in fact, be of the same colour and weight as the fabric.

Three-sided stitch This is a useful appliqué stitch, and can also be used in straight rows in drawn fabric design. Working from right to left, follow the above diagram. The resulting stitches are double.

Using three-sided stitch Three-sided stitch is a firm and attractive way of joining two fabrics and adding a lace edging. The thread used should be of a similar thickness to the fabric.

Embroidery on tulle
Preparing the tulle
Running stitch
Staggered running stitch

Fig. 1

Fig. 2

Running stitch

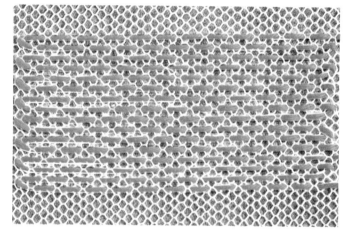

Staggered running stitch

Tulle was first commercially produced in the little town of that name in France. It is a type of net in which the mesh forms a honeycomb pattern. Very fine embroidery can be worked on this base to give a delicate lacy effect. The work requires great care and precision when forming the stitches as the tulle is so transparent that mistakes are very obvious.

Preparing the tulle   1. There are many types of tulle (cotton, silk, nylon) with small, medium or large mesh. Use only fine tulle of the highest quality – to check this, insert a bodkin into the weave which should enlarge without stretching. Use a needle with a rounded tip. The embroidery can be worked over counted threads or by following a pattern drawn on paper, either as an all-over design or as a border. Work is carried out in the three directions shown in **Fig. 1**: **A** is vertical, **B** is horizontal and **C** is diagonal.

2. Draw the pattern with permanent ink on paper or firm cloth. To avoid making the tulle dirty, turn the paper over. The pattern will show through on the reverse side and can still be easily followed. Attach the paper or firm cloth to the tulle with basting stitches of the correct tension. Start the work by stitching round the outline of the design with running stitch, then complete it with the chosen stitches. **Fig. 2** shows how the needle slides over the paper without stitching into it. Remove the paper when the work is finished.

Running stitch   Running stitch is used for outlining a design, but is also the simplest way of covering a background. In the example it is worked in rows back and forth. The stitches are worked in columns, one above the other, giving a soft, regular relief pattern.

Staggered running stitch   This stitch is also worked horizontally. In this case, however, stagger the stitches in each row to give a different effect from the previous stitch.

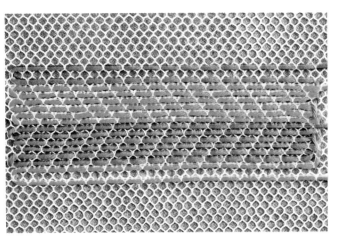

Diagonal running stitch Work diagonally, on every other row of threads. In each row the running stitch is worked over one thread and under one thread of the tulle. In the example two colours have been used, going through alternate holes, but only one may be used if preferred. This produces a firm border.

Simple woven stitch This is worked in running stitch, staggering each row by one thread. Covering all the holes in the tulle in this way gives the fabric a woven appearance. It is especially useful for borders and bolder areas of work.

Alternating woven stitch This is a classic border stitch. Work the diagonal lines first. Start at the right of the work, and in rows back and forth, work the first section. Then continue with the second diagonal section without a break and so on. Use the weave of the tulle alternately to stagger the stitches. Next, fill the gaps, changing to horizontal running stitch and pulling the thread through gently. The final result is a contrast of light and shade, which can also be worked in a single colour.

Darning stitch This is a stitch which creates a good relief effect, using a soft, colourful thread. It can be worked in three directions, vertical, horizontal and diagonal. Work the first row in running stitch, then return along the same row of holes but alternating the stitches. In this stitch it is important not to pull the thread too tightly.

Preparing the work This is a method of embroidery in which small beads or sequins are sewn onto fabric following a traced design. In some cases, especially if the fabric is very delicate, it is best to trace the design onto tissue paper and baste this to the fabric with small stitches. Start the bead work along the outer lines. Carefully tear away the paper from the finished section, and then begin another area. This is because it would be difficult to remove all the paper when the work is finished.

Attaching beads with back stitch This is the most traditional and widely used method. Choose a needle and thread fine enough to thread through the selected beads. The thread should be as strong as possible. Bring the thread through to the right side of the fabric, thread the bead and secure it with a back stitch. Thread another bead and so on, following the traced line. The beads can be closely spaced or further apart, depending on the length of the stitch.

Superimposed beads 1 For maximum effect the beads can be superimposed, one on top of another. Bring the needle through to the right side of the work, thread one bead and then another. Thread through the first bead again and secure with a back stitch. Come out at a chosen distance and stitch another pair of beads.

Superimposed beads 2 Using the method described above, an even greater effect can be achieved by superimposing three beads on top of the first. A small trefoil can be made using beads of various colours.

Grouped beads The beads can also be attached in a row of various colours and groupings. Work a series of beads so that gaps are left for beads of another colour (**A**). Fill in the second section (**B**) and then the third (**C**). For a balanced result, calculate in advance the size of the gaps and the number of beads required.

Embroidery with beads and sequins

Bugle beads	Spaced sequins
Superimposed sequins	Sequins with beads
Fringes of beads and sequins	Sequin flowers

Bugle beads There is no particular method of stitching bugle beads to fabric. Simply thread the beads onto the needle and stitch them into place, carefully judging the length of the stitches. Using bugle beads, it is possible to make zigzag patterns.

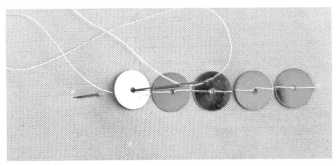

Spaced sequins Bring the thread through to the right side of the fabric, thread the sequin and stitch to the right, coming out on the left of the sequin. Stitch back into the centre and out again to the left, ready to stitch the second sequin.

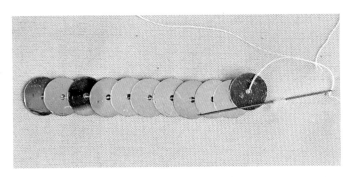

Superimposed sequins Bring the thread through to the right side of the work, thread a sequin onto the needle and make a small back stitch in the fabric to the right as shown. Thread a second sequin onto the needle and make another small back stitch through the fabric to the right. Continue in this way, so that the sequins overlap.

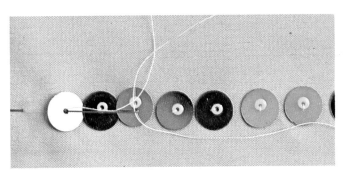

Sequins with beads This is a way of attaching a sequin with a bead at the centre. Bring the thread through to the right side of the work. Pass the thread through the hole in the centre of the sequin and then add a bead. Pass the needle back through the sequin. Stitch through the fabric to the left, to the position of the next sequin.

Fringes of beads and sequins Thread the sequin onto the thread, followed by a number of beads (in this case seven). Pass the thread back through six beads and the sequin and secure them all with a small stitch.

Sequin flowers To achieve this decorative effect, choose sequins which are slightly concave. Thread in order 1 sequin, 1 bead, 1 sequin, 1 bead, 1 sequin, 1 bead, and secure them all with a small stitch. Work round in a circle.

Basic needlepoint stitches
Half cross stitch   Half cross stitch over tramming
Tent stitch   Backing pattern of tent stitch

Half cross stitch Working from left to right, bring the needle up through the canvas and make a small diagonal stitch, going in one hole up and to the right. Come out again one hole vertically downwards. Continue to the end of the row. Turn the work completely upside down for the return row, again working from left to right.

Half cross stitch over tramming Here the half cross stitch is worked over lines of tramming threads which are stitched along the horizontal canvas threads, overlapping about every 12cm (4¾in). This pads out the stitches to achieve good coverage of the canvas.

Tent stitch Working from right to left, bring the needle through to the right side and make a diagonal stitch, going in one hole up and to the right. Come out again on the bottom row one hole further to the left. Continue to the end of the row. Turn the canvas completely upside down and work the next row in the same way, again from right to left.

Backing pattern of tent stitch Long slanting stitches are formed on the back of the canvas with tent stitch. This makes a more durable finish than half cross stitch. However, compared with diagonal tent stitch (see opposite page), this stitch pulls the canvas out of shape more.

Basic needlepoint stitches
Diagonal tent stitch
Backing pattern of diagonal tent stitch
Web stitch

Diagonal tent stitch   1. This method of working tent stitch is in diagonal lines. When working from top to bottom, the needle is held vertically. Make a diagonal stitch over one intersection of canvas, then bring the needle out two holes vertically downwards to begin the next diagonal stitch.

2. When working the next row from bottom to top, the needle is held horizontally. Make a diagonal stitch over one intersection of canvas, then bring the needle out two holes to the left to begin the next stitch. The rows of diagonal stitches interlock.

Backing pattern of diagonal tent stitch This stitch produces a firm backing pattern which looks woven and is more durable than half cross and tent stitch. It has the added advantage of pulling the canvas out of shape less.

Web stitch Lay a tramming thread diagonally from bottom left to top right, then work back down it with diagonal stitches over one canvas intersection. On the next row, work the diagonal stitches so they alternate with those in the previous row, leaving the tramming thread showing in between.

Vertical needlepoint stitches
Upright Gobelin stitch   Brick stitch
Hungarian stitch   Parisian stitch

Upright Gobelin stitch This is a classic stitch with infinite varia-tions. It is stitched over two or three threads. Work from left to right and vice-versa. Make a vertical stitch upwards over three threads of the canvas, coming out on the slant and one thread to the right (or to the left on the return row). Continue in this way until the work is completed.

Brick stitch Work from left to right and vice-versa. Make a vertical stitch upwards over three threads of the canvas. Come out three threads down and two to the right. Continue to the end of the row. On the return row, fill in the gaps between the stitches of the previous row with more vertical stitches over three threads, but overlapping the row above by one thread. Repeat the first and second rows until the work is completed.

Hungarian stitch Work from left to right and vice-versa. Bring the thread through to the right side of the canvas and stitch up over two threads. Move one thread to the right and one down, and make a vertical stitch over four threads. Move one thread to the right and one thread higher than the previous stitch, and make another vertical stitch over two threads. Move two threads to the right and repeat these stitches to the end of the row. The following row is worked in a contrasting colour to interlock with the row above.

Parisian stitch Work in horizontal rows from left to right, and vice-versa. The first row is worked with alternately one vertical stitch over one thread of the canvas and one over three threads, leaving one thread between each stitch. In the following rows the long stitches coincide with the short stitches and vice-vérsa. Use a contrasting colour on alternate rows.

Vertical needlepoint stitches

| Parisian stitch variation | Chevron stitch | Mosaic diamond stitch |
| Diagonal straight stitch | Gobelin variation | Vertical bands |

Parisian stitch variation Work the first row by stitching over four threads, and then over another four, two threads lower. Work the second line of stitches to correspond, but a whole row lower. These two rows form bands, leaving spaces between them. In the second stage, these are filled with small straight stitches over two threads in a contrasting colour.

Chevron stitch The long vertical stitches are worked over four threads in a zigzag pattern, ascending or descending one thread at a time. The spaces between the rows are filled with short vertical stitches worked over two threads in a contrasting colour.

Mosaic diamond stitch This pattern is worked over two, four and six threads to form small diamond shapes. The stitch shows up well if the colour changes with each row.

Diagonal straight stitch The stitches are worked vertically and staggered by one thread every stitch. Start the work at the top left-hand corner and work diagonally down to the right, finishing at the end of the area to be covered. This diagonal serves as a guide for further rows. Work these rows from right to left and vice-versa.

Gobelin variation Work from left to right and vice-versa. Make vertical stitches upwards over one or two threads, coming out one thread to the right (or one to the left on the return row). Blocks of contrasting colours form a chevron pattern.

Vertical bands This is worked in groups of three vertical stitches, each staggered by one thread as shown. Each band changes colour. The bands can be made wider by working more than three stitches across.

Slanting needlepoint stitches
Oblique Gobelin stitch   Alternating slanting Gobelin stitch
Stem stitch   Fern stitch

Oblique Gobelin stitch This is a classic tapestry stitch, worked over two or three threads in height. Work only from left to right, turning the work at the end of each row. Work each stitch slanting one thread to the right, then stitch vertically down, picking up two or three threads of the canvas as shown.

Alternating slanting Gobelin stitch Work in rows from left to right, turning the work on the return row. Work each slanting stitch over three threads of the canvas in height and two threads to the right. On the return row, alternate the stitches to interlock with those of the previous row.

Stem stitch Work from top to bottom and vice-versa. Bring the thread through at the top left-hand corner and make a diagonal stitch down over two threads of the canvas, coming out one thread below the start of the first stitch. Finish the row in this way. On the return row, work from bottom to top, making the stitches symmetrical with those in the first row. When this stage of the work is finished, work small back stitches between the rows, using a finer thread in a contrasting colour.

Fern stitch Work from top to bottom, starting at the top left-hand corner of the work. Stitch diagonally down to the right over two threads, coming out one thread horizontally to the left as shown. Now make an upward diagonal stitch to the right over two threads of the canvas, coming out one thread below the first stitch. Continue in this way to the end of the row, finish off and restart the successive rows.

Knotted stitch Work from left to right. Bring the needle through at the bottom left of the work, make a slanting stitch to the right over three threads up and one to the right. Come out two threads of the canvas vertically down. Make a small diagonal tying stitch one thread up to the left and come out one thread to the right of the initial stitch.

Oriental stitch variation Work diagonally from top to bottom, starting at the top left-hand corner of the work. Stitch diagonally over one thread, then over two, three and four threads, making a small triangle. Now make a series of slanting stitches over two threads of the canvas, first from top to bottom and then from left to right from the triangle in the corner. Fill in the angle made in this way with another small triangle and so on.

Diagonal stitch Work diagonally in rows from left to right and from bottom to top and vice-versa. The first and the fifth stitches in each pattern cover one thread, the second and the fourth cover two threads, while the third, central stitch covers three. On the return row work the stitch covering three threads below the stitch covering only one thread, and so on.

Milanese stitch Start work in the top left-hand corner, working in rows of back stitch back and forth. Having filled in the corner with a diagonal triangle, work a row of diagonal stitches, alternating first over one thread, then over four. In the second row, under each stitch covering one thread, work one which covers two threads, and under each stitch covering four threads, work one which covers three. In the third row, under each stitch covering two threads, work one which covers three threads, and under each stitch covering three threads, work one which covers two. Repeat these rows to produce a series of interlocking triangles.

Renaissance stitch　Work rows back and forth from left to right and vice-versa. Bring the thread through to the right side of the canvas and stitch vertically down over four threads. Bring the needle back out two threads up and one to the left. Make a horizontal tying stitch to the right over one thread and come out one thread to the left of the first stitch as shown.

Alternating Renaissance stitch　This is a simple variation of Renaissance stitch. Leave a space between each vertical stitch which is filled in successive rows. The horizontal tying stitch is worked over two threads. Work in two colours to show the alternating rows.

Florentine or Diagonal mosaic stitch　This is worked in diagonal rows from left to right and from top to bottom and vice-versa. The first diagonal stitch covers a single thread of canvas and the second stitch covers two. On the return row, the long stitch meets the short one in the previous row. Using two colours on alternate rows gives a diagonal striped effect.

Rococo stitch　The vertical stitches are worked over four threads of canvas, the horizontal tying stitches over two. Bring the needle through at the starting point and make a vertical stitch. Make another vertical stitch, re-entering at the top of the stitch just made, and coming out two threads down to the right. Make a horizontal stitch two threads to the left, coming out at the bottom of the vertical stitch. Work the other two sides of the diamond symmetrically and slightly looser. The centres of the diamonds are spaced at six-thread intervals. Make the next row of diamonds interlock with the first.

Needlepoint variations
Scottish stitch   Jacquard stitch
Shell stitch   Chain stitch

Scottish stitch This is worked in two stages. First make a series of squares using tent stitch and then fill in the squares with blocks of flat stitch worked over one, two and three threads of canvas.

Jacquard stitch This stitch is made up of two different diagonal stitches. The first stage is in tent stitch. Work six horizontal and five vertical stitches, making a series of steps diagonally across the canvas. Leave at least two threads of canvas between each row. The intervening spaces are filled with diagonal straight stitches over two canvas threads.

Shell stitch Work four vertical stitches over four threads of the canvas. Make a horizontal stitch from left to right over the four stitches, gathering them together. Come out at the bottom right and start the next group of stitches. For the second stage, using a finer thread in a contrasting colour, work a row of back stitches between the rows, over one thread of canvas. Lastly, using the same thread as for the back stitch, thread through the centre of each group of stitches, making spirals.

Chain stitch Bring the thread through to the right side of the fabric and stitch back into the same point, holding the loop made by the thread with the thumb of the left hand. Bring the point of the needle through several threads away into the centre of the loop and pull up. Stitch back each time into the exit point of the stitch just made.

Crossed needlepoint stitches

Simple cross stitch   Alternating cross stitch
Oblong cross stitch   Oblong cross stitch with back stitch

Simple cross stitch This stitch is worked in two rows. In the first row make diagonal stitches from left to right over a chosen number of canvas threads. In the second row, keeping the stitches symmetrical, stitch over those already worked, forming a cross. On canvas this is the ideal stitch for working large motifs from a chart.

Alternating cross stitch This example shows oblong cross stitch over three horizontal threads of canvas and one vertical, and simple cross stitch over one horizontal thread and one vertical. Work in rows from left to right and return from right to left, using the same method as for simple cross stitch. Alternate the position of the crosses in following rows.

Oblong cross stitch Use the same method as for simple cross stitch, but stitching over a greater number of horizontal canvas threads than vertical canvas threads. In this example, the crosses are worked over three horizontal and two vertical threads. Work from left to right for the first stage and from right to left on the return row.

Oblong cross stitch with back stitch Work a row of oblong cross stitch. Next work a row of back stitch so that the stitches cover the intersections of the crosses. Change the colours of the rows to give a bold striped effect.

Smyrna or Double cross stitch Each cross is completed before starting the next, working in rows from left to right. Having made an ordinary cross stitch, the needle is brought through to the right side of the canvas at the centre bottom of the stitch. Make a vertical stitch and come out at the centre right for the horizontal stitch. Stitch up to the right to the starting point of the next stitch.

Greek cross stitch Work from left to right. Start on the left of the work and stitch diagonally up to the right over two threads of canvas. Come out two threads to the left. Stitch down to the right over four vertical threads, and two horizontal. Come out two threads to the left. Continue in this way to the end of the row.

Star or Algerian eye stitch Work in horizontal rows from left to right and vice-versa. The star is worked over four threads of the canvas each way. Bring the needle through at the top left and stitch diagonally down into the centre over two threads. Come out vertically two threads to the right and stitch down into the centre. Work the other six stitches also down into the centre, alternating a diagonal with a horizontal or a vertical.

Rice stitch or Crossed corners Work fairly large cross stitches to cover the surface of the canvas. This example uses four threads of the canvas each way. Then, with a contrasting colour, tie down the diagonals with a row of smaller diagonal stitches over two threads. First make a row from left to right. On the return row, work from right to left, filling the gaps left in the first row. It is usual to use a light colour on a dark background.

Florentine work
Symmetrical flame stitch
Modern flame stitch

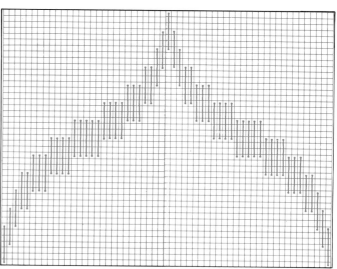

Symmetrical flame stitch 1. This decorative stitch, which takes its name from the pattern formed by the stepped blocks of vertical stitches, resembles tongues of flame. The first row of stitching follows an undulating line and must be counted out carefully from a chart. The successive rows all follow this first line.

2. Symmetrical flame stitch is worked from left to right and vice-versa, following the pattern on the chart (see above). The pattern is continuous and the stitches are all the same height. The stitches are worked from top to bottom with the needle held on a slant, and moving one thread to the left (or right) with each stitch. The stitches are vertical on the right side of the work and slanting on the reverse. In the second and following rows, the stitches fit into the top or bottom of the stitches of the foundation row.

Modern flame stitch 1. Use the same method as described for symmetrical flame stitch. If a regular effect is desired, start at the centre of the work, and work to the left and right of this point. In this example the stitches are spaced so that they intersect one another as in brick stitch.

2. Working in rows from left to right and vice-versa, follow the pattern from the chart above. To achieve a good result, choose a selection of contrasting colours. The best effects are achieved by shading the colours from light to dark and vice-versa. Flame stitch needlepoint, either traditional or modern, can be used to cover stools, period chairs, small objects such as boxes etc, and cushion covers.

Florentine work
Irregular flame stitch
Asymmetrical flame stitch

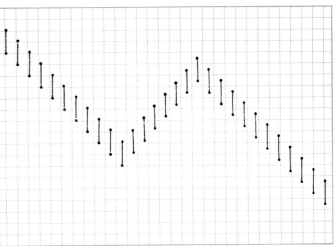

Irregular flame stitch 1. Flame stitch usually follows a symmetrical pattern, but the following example is for an irregular zigzag. The pattern is repeated but the zigzag line drops down to the right. This method is used in modern work, in place of the traditional versions of flame stitch.

2. Work the first row from left to right over two threads of canvas, following the chart shown above. This pattern is most pleasing when each colour is used in several tones.

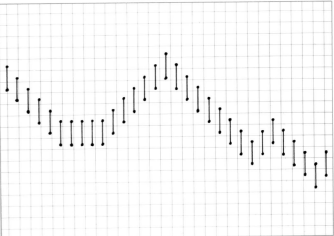

Asymmetrical flame stitch 1. This sequence of stitches, as in the previous example, follows a zigzag line. The stitches are worked over two threads of canvas.

2. Follow the pattern on the chart above, and repeat it across the work, making an asymmetrical but continuous design. Having worked the first row, the following rows fit in above and below.

Decorative needlepoint patterns

Dot stitch   Swiss stitch
Flower stitch   Zigzag stitch
Basket stitch   Bow stitch

Dot stitch

Swiss stitch

Flower stitch

Zigzag stitch

Basket stitch

Bow stitch

Decorative needlepoint patterns

Arrow stitch   Wave stitch   Flame stitch variation
Step stitch   Lightning stitch   Pine stitch
   Diamond stitch   Beehive stitch

Arrow stitch

Flame stitch variation

Step stitch

Pine stitch

Wave stitch

Lightning stitch

Diamond stitch

Beehive stitch

189

INDEX

Many stitches have the same name whether used in crochet (c), embroidery (e), knitting (k), or needlepoint (n). In order to make it clear which stitch is indexed therefore, a signifying letter is used for each entry.

CREDITS
Endpapers, p.66 and p.128 – Robert Harding Picture Library
p.8 – Jacqui Hurst